THE UK SCRIPTWRITER'S
SURVIVAL
HANDBOOK

(or How to Earn an Actual Living as a Writer)

BY TIM CLAGUE
& DANNY STACK

Plus quotes and insights from other writers
we've met, or heard in talks and conferences

Foreword by Tony Jordan

Illustrated by Emily Gilbert

http://emilygilbertillustration.com/

FOREWORD

By Tony Jordan

Becoming a screenwriter is as tough in the UK as it is everywhere else in the world, maybe even more so. Our film and television output has a well-deserved reputation for quality, both in its writing and in its production values.

As in every industry, the toughest part is getting your first break, your foot on the first rung of the ladder; only once that's happened can you learn how far your talent as a writer can take you. Yet, even once you get on the ladder, the journey to your first BAFTA is still a difficult one, learning to navigate your way through the industry, whilst trying to hold on to the most important thing you possess as a writer. Your unique voice.

In this book, Tim and Danny have put together some great tips for surviving the process. Good luck!

Tony Jordan
Writer/Producer
Former Head Writer on *EastEnders*
Writer/Creator of *Hustle*
Co-creator of *Life On Mars*

A HANDY GUIDE TO THE HANDBOOK

FADE IN

To make it as a scriptwriter, a working writer, a writer who gets paid, you need to have the right attitude and approach. This handbook is going to break down practical and proactive techniques to help you get started, and show you how to maintain a career once you're up and running.

It's a book that's less about the craft of *scriptwriting* and more about being a *working* scriptwriter. A writer who earns a crust day-to-day. A writer who pays the rent *and* still finds time to work on new ideas, and that next amazing spec script.

There are lots of books about rare occurrences of someone "selling it big". This book is about being part of the hard-working majority, not a one-off fluke. If you picked up a book about investing your money, you'd be rightly disappointed if the advice inside was "win the lottery". There'll be no "sell a script for a million dollars on your first go" nonsense here. This book is about long-term success through graft.

We work in the UK and this book refers to a lot of advice that is UK-based. But the underlying ideas work anywhere. If you follow the advice in this handbook, we're confident you'll see better results in your writing career. It will influence not only what you achieve, but also how you achieve it. No rules, no formulas, just a lot of common sense and a full commitment to the cause. We're going to flip a cliché and reinvent it: it's not necessarily *who* you know, it's *what* you know, and *how* you use it.

> There's a secret easy path to being a successful writer. All you have to do is to work really really hard, write good stuff and keep sending it out and keep rewriting and keep learning. And it only takes five to ten years!

James Moran
Writer
Doctor Who, Torchwood, Severance, Cockneys Vs Zombies

TIM AND DANNY WHO?

We're not big famous writers. We're not academics

either. We're a couple of writers and filmmakers who make a living out of what we do. We both feel we've taken some wrong turns in the past, mainly because things worked differently to how we were told or how we thought they would turn out. This is why we feel this book is essential, to expose some misconceptions and be honest about what the process is really like.

Tim

Tim Clague wrote the BAFTA-nominated short film *Eight*, the story of a young boy's quest to find out about his dad. Since then he has written and directed an array of short films that have screened at international festivals and won awards. Tim also has broadcast credits with ITV and BBC.

His focus is on new techniques and new technologies across a range of formats and genres. He created the popular comedy web series *Mr Vista*. He was Senior Creative Designer (senior writer) on the large-scale PC game *APB*. He has written and directed corporate films, adverts and e-learning material, with budgets of up to £300,000.

As a team, Tim and Danny have worked on the UK Scriptwriters podcast, screenwriting talks, adverts and corporate films. They have taken their collaboration one step further by co-writing, producing and directing the live-action children's film *Who Killed Nelson Nutmeg?*

Visit the film's website
http://nelsonnutmeg.com
Twitter - @nelsonnutmeg

Visit the UK Scriptwriters podcast
http://ukscriptwriters.podomatic.com
Twitter - @ukscriptwriters

Danny

Danny's TV writing credits include *EastEnders*, *Doctors* and high-profile children's shows such as *Octonauts* and *Roy* (both CBBC), and *Thunderbirds Are Go!* for CiTV. He also writes and directs. His supernatural thriller, *Origin*, won Best

Horror at the London Independent Film Festival in 2012. He script edited the feature films *The Man Inside* and *Kings*, and for many years was a story analyst for film companies such as Working Title, Pathé, Miramax and UK Film Council. He writes the popular blog, *Scriptwriting in the UK*, which inspired him to set up the Red Planet Prize, a scheme to discover new writers, with writer/producer Tony Jordan.

SEVEN CORNERSTONES OF SURVIVAL

If you're going to take anything away from this handbook, then these **7 cornerstones of survival** will see you right. Understand these principles and you can cope with new and unexpected events as they arise.

1 – Be in it for the long term

Writing a feature takes time. Writing a TV episode is a lot of work. Even a good short film isn't something you can just bang out. It normally takes four or five pieces of work before a writer finds their original voice. Becoming a good writer isn't a fast process. We're talking about years, not months. It takes time to build your network, to get experienced at pitching, to weave excellent loglines and outlines. Whichever way you look at it, becoming a good, profitable writer in a short space of time is unlikely. The advice we share in this book is simple. You can start using it straight away, today. We know it works. Yet we also know that the best writers get better at using these ideas over time.

> *I'm not that clever, but what I am is unbelievably tenacious. It's my tenacity that has allowed me to have a good career.*

Lord Puttnam
Producer and Studio Executive

2 – It's a small industry

The industry's huge, right? Impenetrable and overwhelming, yes? After all, there are thousands of people constantly trying to get their break, not to mention thousands already working within the system.

In terms of finding the right people to work with, the industry thrives on referrals and recommendations. For the new writer, this means it's important to make a good impression, no matter whom you meet or where and when you meet them.

This is actually a small industry. Reputations count. The industry likes to work with talented people, but being nice and reliable can go a long way, too. It's hard work, working with someone who's a pain in the backside.

A very experienced salesman, a millionaire in fact, once said to me: "Always tell the truth to everyone. They share notes. And you're not clever enough to remember what lies you told to which person."

3 – There is no "inside"

Remember poor old Gil from *The Simpsons*, the Jack Lemmon-style salesman always looking for that one sale that will "make ol' Gil some green"? Sometimes writers feel the same. "Come on, just one script option, then ol' Writer here will get their big break."

This "big break" mentality is a fallacy. It can force you to think of the industry as a ring-fenced citadel with you on the outside and "them" on the inside. They've got everything and you've got nothing – and if only they recognised your talent, they would invite you in, too.

Where has this "inside" vision come from? Most likely

from the media's portrayal of itself! It likes news stories about people who come from nowhere and then are "in" the biz! That's good copy, but it's not how things work for 90% of people.

The industry is just a collection of people trying to get by, just like you. They don't have secret meetings about keeping people out. If you focus on individuals within the system rather than imagining a big industry citadel with a single key, you'll be better off.

4 – Do it your way, today

Don't spend too long comparing yourself to others. Their path to success won't be the same as yours. Sure, pick up some tips and inspiration, but everyone's journey is different. Everyone's motivations come from a different heart. Everyone has their own voice.

Don't think: "Well, Richard Curtis built his career by steps 1, 2, 3 – I will do the same." But his career grew out of his life; it was built up from his contacts, and the people he worked with strengthened it. Your life, contacts and colleagues are, and will be, different. Use what you have.

5 – Don't wait to be invited

Too many writers wait to be invited. They seek permission to be a writer. They ask agents to let them be writers. They enter competitions to win the right to be seen as a writer. They beg producers: "Please let me write something that you can then own."

Instead, what if all that effort was used to actually make something: to do your own work, to produce your own short film, to write something that doesn't need a lot of money to make, to team up with other people at your level? We've got a whole chapter dedicated to ideas you might try. For now, we want to leave you with the overall idea that it's time to get busy, and to take matters into your own hands.

6 – Life is not a meritocracy

The best people don't always rise to the top. The best scripts don't always win competitions. The best writer doesn't always get the gig. Who decides what "best" means anyway? And are they the best person to do it? And on it goes.

When things go right, it's often because of hard work and talent. But luck plays a part, too. Don't forget that. You can learn to work harder, improve your skills, and develop new techniques. Luck is just luck, there's not much you can do about that. It's important to put things in perspective and stick to what matters most: your writing and your career.

7 – Think about things from the other side

Producers, execs and script editors are busy people, with constant demands on their time. If you contact them hoping to solicit a script request or get some work, then put yourself in their shoes and try to examine your approach from their point of view.

Do you have a script that's relevant to the type of film or show they like to make? Have you researched their credits and background? Are you making a generic cold call just looking for a break? Why should the producer/exec/script editor care? What's different about you? Why should they reply to your email or take your call? Think about what they want, and how you can respond to their needs and routine.

BONUS – The good news

Writing stories for any medium is the best job in the world. Before a writer comes along, there's nothing. There's a blank sheet of paper or, at best, some scrappy notes. When you hand over a script, there's a world inhabited by original characters involved in dramatic and funny situations. It's very, very cool, and it's all thanks to the writer.

A few years ago, the Writers Guild of America ran a campaign called *Somebody Wrote That* (designed by Scott Roeben) that neatly summed it up. It shows us those defining moments, those great characters, those crazy gags, and those touching scenes that affect us the most – and reminds us that a writer was behind them. Actors can say the lines, directors can make the action jump off the screen, editors can fine-tune a sequence and give it impact. But before all that, the writer had the idea and wrote the story. It's a privileged position, and an awesome place to be.

> Special effects and so on come and go. That's fashion. Writers aren't in the fashion business. They are in the eternity business.

Lord Puttnam

8.3 million viewers watched my first episode of EastEnders. 8.3 million! I mean, 8.3 million! Eight. Point. Three. Million. I can't even begin to imagine that number of people. I need to sit down.

My best experience as a writer was small, yet powerful. A girl called Amy came up to me at a Future Shorts screening to say how much Eight (my BAFTA-nominated short film) had meant to her and she had organised screenings of it in her home town. That to me is the power of the writer – creating stories that resonate with people.

SURVIVAL – TOP TIPS

A recap of this chapter

1 – Be in it for the long term

There's no quick-win method for a long career.

2 – It's a small industry

Be nice to people, they will remember you.

3 – There is no "inside"

The industry is just people, like you.

4 – Do it your way, today

Play to your own strengths, don't copy.

5 – Don't wait to be invited

Start making stuff, you don't need permission.

6 – Life is not a meritocracy

The best doesn't always get picked. Live with it.

7 – Think about the other side

How would you like to be treated? Do that.

STARTING OUT

It doesn't matter if you're a screenwriting graduate or a middle-aged housewife, young or old, male or female, what matters is that you've written a script (or two, or heck, even more). And now you're ready to take the industry by storm. But where do you start? What do you do?

- Don't approach an agent yet.
- Get independent feedback on your script(s) to see if it's any good. *Note: don't get feedback from friends and family.*
- Soak up the feedback. Rewrite script(s) as necessary.
- Don't approach an agent yet. You're not ready.
- Once you're happy with your rewrite and confident the script's the best it can be, consider putting it through "the system".
- Don't approach an agent yet. YOU'RE NOT READY. Really.

THE THREE P's

Practical. Proactive. Professional. These three P's are useful to think about at the start of your career.

Practical

A writing career doesn't happen overnight, as we've already said. You've got to "be in it for the long term". If you've decided to take the plunge and live the dream, then that's great. It's very  exciting. It's also horrendously daunting.

Look at your practical options. How are you going to make money while you build your writing portfolio to such a standard that you earn money from writing? Do you take a part-time job (likely) or can you get an industry-related part-time job like script reading or script editing (preferable, but harder to achieve)?

Domestic issues will vary from person to person (partner, kids, illness, disability, etc.) but you should ask yourself: "What is the very basic income I need to survive? How am I going to achieve that?" Once these essential concerns are dealt with, then all effort can be focused on writing. But make sure you're applying your energy in the right areas, like new writing opportunities, entry-level TV, short films, and using all relevant contacts to nab potential writing gigs (corporate, commercial, radio, theatre, internet).

The key thing is that you find a proper practical solution that is "your way".

Proactive

A lot of writing opportunities will emerge not just because of what you know and the quality of your writing, but because of *who* you know and the broad appeal of your personality. Get out there. Attend industry events. Make contacts. Start a blog or a Twitter feed, or set up a dedicated Facebook writing page. Be friendly, supportive and positive. Don't expect opportunities to come to your door. Go out and find them yourself. Remember, "don't wait to be invited".

Professional

Take responsibility for your writing. It's not "them", it's

"you". The system doesn't suck. The system exists for itself. In the process, professional courtesies may fall between the cracks. Sometimes it may be understandable, occasionally it may be rude, while other times it may be plain unforgivable. Get on with it. As we've said already, "life is not a meritocracy". Let off steam with friends and fellow writers, but don't burn bridges as "it's a small industry". Don't take rejections personally. Take criticism on board, but keep it in perspective. Stick to your convictions. Be assured about what you want to say. Develop your original voice. Realise the strengths of your writing and try to understand the weaker areas so that you can develop a balanced critique of your own material. Keep writing. Get your work out there. You never know what's going to stick – where and with whom. Now, how much do you want it? Really? What are you prepared to do? Then do it.

And now, a fourth P. Patience.

It's going to take time. There's going to be a lot of rejection and frustration that, hopefully, will be worth it for one or two moments of

elation or validation that will kick-start a writing career. But it doesn't get easier. It gets harder. Competition is fierce. Opportunities are few and far between. Don't get complacent or bitter. Stay focused. Keep writing. Take inspiration from your favourite films and TV shows, and the success stories of your peers. Be wary of writer envy. There's no right way to go about it except by writing consistently good material. That's what it's all about. Your unique talent. Hopefully that will be enough to earn you a living, and give you the foothold you need to make all your dreams come true.

REMEMBER
Do it your way, today

THE UNSOLICITED MATERIAL CONUNDRUM

You don't have a credit – and yet you need a credit to get your script read. An agent would help, but they don't take on writers with no credits! What?! The whole world is against you. But you know that can't be true, as we've already told you that "there is no inside".

How do you get around this unsolicited material conundrum?

* The *Writers' & Artists' Yearbook* lists a huge number of production companies and usually mentions if they accept unsolicited material or not. But here's the thing: *everybody* accepts unsolicited material, even if they say they don't. The trick is to make contact with the assistant,

exec, co-ordinator, whoever, either via email or the phone, and convince them you're a lovely normal person who has a promising script to read. Show a bit of charm and hustle, and no door will be closed to you.

Visit the *Writers' & Artists' Yearbook*
https://www.writersandartists.co.uk

- For TV scripts, submit to the BBC writersroom. They have a few submission windows a year. See their website for full details, and other opportunities such as their TV shadow schemes (for *Holby City*, *Casualty*, *EastEnders* and *Doctors*). See also our Competitions section.

Visit the BBC writersroom
http://www.bbc.co.uk/writersroom/

- For film scripts, research the production companies that are most relevant to the genre of your script. There's no point sending your superhero movie to a company that only makes low-budget crime thrillers.

- Write a good query/approach letter or email. Be brief but not too dry or formal. Three paragraphs should do it: first to introduce yourself, then the logline of your latest script, and a final paragraph on how your script suits the production company and asking them if they'd like to read it. There's more on making an approach in the chapter "Reaching Out".

- Alternatively, phone the production company. Speak to the assistant and/or receptionist. *Be nice*. Charming, too, if you can. Ask if you can submit your script, or email the producer/exec directly.

- Submit your script for BFI development funding, although it's preferable to have a producer/production company attached to increase your chances of being awarded funding. See the BFI's website for full details as their awards and schemes change often.

- Attend film festivals, talks, seminars, etc. Get to know fellow writers. Find out about script editors. Put your name out there. This makes you more agreeable and identifiable when you take the unsolicited approach – they will have heard of you.

- A referral or recommendation to an agent or a producer about you and your work is a great boost. In 2009, Danny referred Kevin Lehane to an exec he knew (because Kevin's scripts were good and he'd worked on one of Danny's short films for free), and next minute, Kevin's in the trades, nabbing an agent, making sales, *and* getting his film, *Grabbers*, made. Hey, what do you know, the system works!

NO ONE COMES FROM NOWHERE

The news media is fond of "overnight success" stories. You know the type: "Two young men from Gosport are wowing audiences on the big screen with their first ever film – next stop Hollywood."

In truth, this success has been coming for a while, and might go something like this: The two young men from Gosport are a couple of thirty-year-old professionals who have been making award-winning short films for years. They were then selected, out of hundreds of others, to be on the Write Shoot Distribute scheme, and from there they worked hard building up contacts. They wrote four spec feature scripts, one of which worked well as a low-budget feature. However, the financing fell through so they started all over again. This time, they raised enough funding after jumping through a load of hoops or making personal sacrifices (perhaps re-mortgaging their homes!). They finished the film, and it was accepted in an indie film festival, and won the Audience Award for Best Film. This attracted a Hollywood producer who has given them a tentative offer to develop one of their spec scripts. There's no money yet, so for now they're hoping to get some TV directing work to tide themselves over.

Even though this is a fabricated example, it's in fact quite common with the type of overnight success stories that you may see. The point is: **no one comes from nowhere.**

When you achieve some level of success or recognition, you won't have come from nowhere either. So, do the hard work. Get

REMEMBER
Be in it for the long term

better. Dig deeper. Refine your craft. Learn from the mistakes. And in ten years' time, you too can be an overnight success!

BE READY

When your overnight success opportunity taps you on the shoulder, will you be ready? Are you ready to hit the ground running?

KEY ADVICE: Always have projects on the go, and at various stages of development. One script will not a career make. You're a writer, you're an ideas person, so you probably have a lot of ideas. But get them out of your head and onto the page where they will do some good.

I won the Jerwood Film Prize in 1999 and gained my BAFTA nomination. I had a lot of meetings with agents and production companies. "What's next?" they would ask. I was 25 at the time. I had some feature ideas, but had never written a feature. So I wrote a script, but it was a typical first feature attempt full of naive mistakes. For me it was too early, I wasn't ready. But this experience taught me a valuable lesson. Since then, I'm always ready for "what's next?"

PUT EVERYTHING INTO EVERYTHING

When I was starting out I was mainly working on corporate projects, and doing spec writing in the evenings. Inside, my approach was something like: "I really want to be a filmmaker, so I will put my creativity into the spec scripts. I'll do the minimum on the corporate work to save my energy. No point in using up the good stuff on that."

This is totally the wrong approach, for three reasons:

1 - Creativity is an infinite resource. You don't "use it up". In fact, the opposite is true. The more you use it, the stronger it grows.

2 - People who are successful in one field tend to be successful in another. Investors like to invest in people who have proven themselves and do profitable work.

3 - *All* your work is your calling card. If you can't be trusted to put 100% into a little piece of corporate work, why would someone think you would do it on a feature film?

We know how easy it can be to look around at the world of UK film and TV, and the people who inhabit it, and think: "Cuh, they've got it good" or "It must be easy for them" or "Why are they getting ahead, what's so good about them?"

This casual frustration can develop into negative cynicism: "The industry's too closed off", "It doesn't do enough to help new writers", "It's just a load of egos."

In many ways, the industry is a passive beast that just reacts to what happens around it. It will respond warmly to your success rather than create the success for you. This means *you* are in control of the work that's going to get you noticed. Sure, it

REMEMBER
There is
no 'inside'

helps to get industry support every now and then (see Competitions section in the next chapter), but the baseline of any emerging writer should be to keep doing the work that most excites them rather than strategically trying to attract industry interest. When you follow the work that most excites you, the industry will come to you – or at least be aware of you – because of the momentum you've created from your own endeavour.

How do you create this endeavour?

You get busy. You write.

But now you have to do more. You have to get busy creating content. Go beyond the script. Produce something or get something made.

Even if you've no interest in producing or directing, you can still find people to fill these roles.

There should be nothing stopping you from staging your own play at a hired venue; writing and recording a radio play; making a short film, or better yet, making a low-budget feature. If (no, *when*) you create this content, and it's good, it will generate a buzz and possibly go on to attract press interest and/or awards (no matter how small).

Remember, the internet is ours. We own it. We're responsible for the content. Or at least we *can* be. We don't have to be passive consumers making glib comments on Facebook or snide asides on Twitter.

- If you've never made a web series, why haven't you?
- Have you considered getting your mates to perform scenes from your script, just to see if they're working? Or using a scene as a teaser for people to watch?
- Do you write a blog? Why not?

A new writer in the 21st century will struggle if they stick solely to what's on the page. We deal in a visual medium, and we have the means and resources to visualise our content, so that's what you should be doing. No excuses.

If this idea intrigues, then there's a whole chapter about how to achieve it called "Taking Control".

TIM'S SCRIPTWRITER'S LIFE

A few years ago, Tim created a diagram ("I'm fond of a chart!") to try to capture a writer's working activity. Its original purpose was as a kind of teaching tool for students and graduates. However, it's more often used by writers as an *aide-mémoire*, or as a guide to splitting up their time.

Here it is...

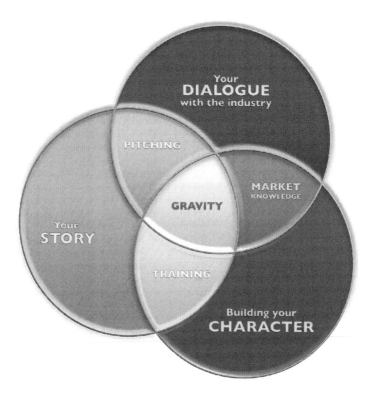

But what does it all mean? Let's start with the three large circles.

Your story

This is your craft, your skills, your writing abilities. Someone who is good at this circle will know how to format a script, is aware of different structures to use, and can call upon many different techniques to write great dialogue. In fact, this is all the stuff we *aren't* covering in this book (i.e. the craft of writing). Interestingly, this is pretty much *all* they teach you on a writing course. It's important, yes, but the practicalities of survival are essential, too.

Your dialogue with the industry

This is about keeping in touch with producers, agents, commissioners and independent content creators. It's about knowing who is doing what and what they're looking for – and about how to present yourself, professionally, to meet those opportunities. Dialogue is two-way, after all.

Building your character

This final circle is the one that writers most often forget about. It concerns your own development, your own growth. It's about looking inwards, reflecting on yourself, as well as looking outwards for new ideas and new sources of inspiration. In short, it's about being an interesting person, so that you write interesting scripts.

Keeping a balance

It's easy to agree with the content of all three circles, and see that each is important. But balance is the key.

For example, some writers may have **no 'story'**. This means they know everyone and know the biz, but they have no craft skills. This kind of writer will do OK in the short term, maybe, by leaning on their contacts. But repeat work will never come, as they can't deliver a high-quality product, reliably and on time, repeatedly.

Writers who have **no 'dialogue'** have a lot of skill in writing and they have interesting things to say. Their scripts are probably excellent and inspiring. It's a tragedy that we'll never see them made because no one in the industry knows about this hidden talent.

Writers who have **no 'character'** have competent scripts and they know the right people in the biz to send them to. But their scripts are generic, a bit lifeless, based only on other films. Without the red circle they have nothing new to say, putting their well-crafted scripts in the "good, but not great" pile again and again.

Overlaps

Some common activities of a writer occur where two of the circles overlap.

For example, pitching involves both your industry knowledge and your storytelling skills. A good pitch demands that you know how your story works, but also how that slots into what the industry wants.

Market knowledge is about reading the trades, about knowing what the right rate is for your work and about the trends in your market.

Sometimes you can lift your skills at the same time as building your own character. This overlap is called "training" – but it includes things like talks, seminars, mentoring, screenwriting festivals and so on.

At the centre, gravity

Get all three circles working for you and you start to build "gravity" almost automatically. Someone with gravity has people who call them, they don't have to chase down work all the time. People are attracted to them. And why wouldn't they be? A person with gravity has talent, is interesting and knows the writing biz.

Go for it – get heavy!

TEN-YEAR PLAN

The commonly referenced amount of time to "make it" as a screenwriter is ten years. This is how long it takes to get your career up and running. Ten years seems like an awfully long time for little or no return on a screenwriting vision. But it doesn't mean that nothing is happening as you toil away year after year. There should be constant and gradual signs of improvement or development, for example: getting an agent, someone giving you a bit of money to develop an idea or write a treatment, getting onto a TV shadow scheme, and so on.

To ensure that these positive developments occur, it's useful to have a **Ten-Year Plan** in mind.

When writing a script it can help if you have an idea of the third act and the resolution before you start. The Ten-Year Plan is simply applying that idea to real life.

Outline specific practical milestones that you would like to happen on your screenwriting journey. You can even break it down into smaller chunks, like the Five-Year Plan or the This Time Next Year I Will... Plan, and use these as the necessary focus to get stuff done.

If you're starting from scratch, then start to break down your goals. Here are some milestones we suggest:

 Write a feature script, or two, and maybe a TV spec as well. Rewrite. Start sending them out when ready. Don't give up the day job.

 Follow up on contacts and leads, enter competitions, make a short film (write, produce or direct), attend networking events. Keep writing and rewriting.

 Get a TV commission – or at least have some good meetings leading up to one. Make another short film. Write new spec scripts. Try to find an agent.

Try to build on the TV commission(s). Get an option on one of your scripts with a reputable production company, and/or decide to make a feature film yourself.

Establish your profile in your chosen field, learning more about your craft and developing your writing skills. Get your feature film made with or without industry backing.

If income/work is taking a dip, don't worry, it's natural. Time for a new writing slate, and that means writing new scripts. Choose a specific area/genre you're best at.

Continue to write and hustle, but now with the benefit of six years' experience. This year, aim to build long-lasting business friendships.

 Enjoy a resurgence of your work and career profile. Keep going. Keep writing. People are now aware of your consistency and progress. Branch out into new areas of writing.

 Funny how the more things change, the more they stay the same. Build your reputation. Aim for several steady, but small, gigs.

 Your financed feature gets made and/or you get offered a TV gig as core writer. Finally, real success! Regular money! Maybe *now*'s the time to give up the day job!

The transition into full-time freelance screenwriter wasn't easy for me. For the first four years, I spent a lot of time focusing on study: reading thousands of scripts, devouring everything in my screenwriting path, immersing myself in screenplay culture.

I managed to option a couple of my scripts and this felt good but hardly reassuring for my bank balance. My break came when I was accepted on to BBC's Doctors (in 2004) and then later that year I won a BBC New Writing Award.

At the time, it felt like all of that was my apprenticeship and only now did my career start in earnest. But it's been ten years since the New Writing Award, so the "ten-year plan" approach has been eerily accurate even though I've been busting a gut to make things happen A LOT sooner.

Choosing a screenwriting career is not an easy life. "Overnight success" takes years to accumulate. Rejection awaits your work on every submission. Confidence takes a regular battering, and an energetic social life – and the income to support it – quickly goes out the window. An interest becomes an obsession and the obsession becomes the career. But the career's going to take time. Do you have ten years to spare?

REMEMBER
Be in it for
the long term

STARTING OUT – TOP TIPS

A recap of this chapter

1 – Get a long-term plan together

We talked about a 10-year plan; you can put your own together.

2 – Develop a balance in your "Scriptwriter's Life"

Don't neglect any of the three circles: your craft, your business contacts or your own personal development.

3 – Live the Three P's

Be practical, proactive and professional.

4 – Remember the fourth P

Patience is also key. No one comes from nowhere.

Classic
Opportunities

These are the scriptwriting opportunities that you may already know about. If you're new to writing, then consider these the "normal" opportunities that most writers start out using. Are they the full picture? No. Are they a good place to start? Yes. And should you know about them and use them? YES!

> If you go to Wembley and you have 90,000 people cheering at once the feeling is overwhelming. Now think that you can make 20 million people do something at the same time. That's television.

Tony Jordan

COMPETITIONS

Competitions, schemes and writing initiatives offer a great opportunity for a new writer to get noticed. New competitions and schemes pop up all the time (equally, some die quickly) but there are a few that have established a decent track record and are still going strong. Schemes that charge a fee usually do so to cover basic admin expenses, reading costs or to add to the winning prize money; a fee doesn't mean they're trying to rip you off. But be sensible. Weigh up the pros and cons of entering, and if there is a fee, check out what you get for your money (e.g. do you get feedback even if you don't win or place in competition?).

Notable competitions/schemes

As mentioned above, these can change quickly. But the list below is correct at the time of going to press. If the exact links don't work, then perhaps search directly online.

* The Red Planet Prize (which Danny helped set up and is now run by Tony Jordan!)
  http://www.redplanetpictures.co.uk/prize.php

* BBC writersroom submissions and opportunities
  http://www.bbc.co.uk/writersroom/opportunities/

- BBC writersroom TV shadow scheme
  http://www.bbc.co.uk/writersroom/about/continuing-drama

- Channel 4's Coming Up
  http://www.touchpapertv.com/productions/coming-up

- Screenwriting Goldmine Awards
  http://awards.screenwritinggoldmine.com/

- British Short Screenplay Competition
  http://www.kaosfilms.co.uk/bssc/

- BAFTA/Rocliffe New Writing Forum
  http://www.bafta.org/about/supporting-talent/rocliffe/

International competitions

- Blue Cat Screenplay Competition
  http://www.bluecatscreenplay.com/

- Nicholl Fellowship (Oscars)
  http://www.oscars.org/awards/nicholl/index.html

- Sir Peter Ustinov TV Scriptwriting Award
  http://www.iemmys.tv/foundation.aspx

- Disney/ABC Writing Fellowship
  http://www.abctalentdevelopment.com/

- PAGE International Screenwriting Awards
  http://pageawards.com/

- Final Draft Big Break Contest
  http://www.finaldraft.com/products/big-break-contest/

> *Execs like to think that writing is somehow magic. They don't want to know what's in the sausage.*

Doug Chamberlin
Writer
Toy Story 2

GET A JOB IN TV

Getting your foot stuck in the swinging doors of UK television is not as impossible as you might imagine. While you might have grand dreams and ambitions of being a BAFTA- or Oscar-winning writer, the humble truth of it is that everyone has to start somewhere.

The opportunistic tales about being spotted or a script being chosen out of the pile above the rest are not about you and are never likely to be. It's like the story of the two lads from Gosport headed for Hollywood glory again!

If you want a career in the UK industry, you just have to get involved. Be prepared to work in a minor role, gain some contacts and then roll the dice to see what happens.

This particularly applies if you're a graduate or someone still in their late teens/early twenties. But it doesn't matter what age you are. If you're fed up with writing to a vacuum from your pad in Poole, then make some effort to be part of the process rather than continually complaining about the system.

> *You can say I've done radio, I've done novels, I've done this, I've done that – but TV writing is seen as the pinnacle. You have to prove you're good enough.*
>
> **Richard Dinnick**
> Children's TV Writer

Like most things, it's a simple enough approach and procedure, but it takes a lot of hard graft, determination and luck to get a break. If you're not doing it, someone else is benefiting.

- Watch the credits of shows that you enjoy. Make a note of the producer's name and the production company which made the programme.
- Write to the producer. Better still, telephone to see if the producer works at the production company full time or if they're freelance. Get to know the assistant. Be polite but don't get chummy. Ask

them about the chances of getting work (as a
runner/PA/whatever) and ask who the best person
to contact is about this.

- Thank them for their time and then write to the
producer. Tell them who you are, that you love
their shows and you want to work for them.

- You won't get a reply. That's OK. Follow it up with
a phone call. Talk to the assistant. They'll
remember you, might like the sound of you and
promise to put your CV on top of the pile. You
might get a call back, an opportunity might crop
up, you never know. But you've just made a
contact with the assistant, and that's the name of
the game.

- Regular TV favourites like *Have I Got News For You*
and *Never Mind the Buzzcocks* (both made by Hat
Trick Productions) seem to have a high turnaround
of staff per season. The runners will move on to
something else or become a researcher, so that
leaves a spot open. Be alert and aware, and pick
the right time to contact.

- The BBC advertise all their jobs through their
website, the national papers and their in-house
magazine, *Ariel* (http://www.bbc.co.uk/ariel/).

- Check out *The Guardian*'s Monday media section
for all sorts of media jobs and opportunities.

- *Broadcast* is the TV industry trade mag for the UK
market. It's astounding how so few people wanting

to break into the biz know of its existence. Get with the programme. It's on sale every Friday and has a regular Appointments page at the back with lots of jobs available, from runner to researcher, AP and producer.

- Channel 4 and Channel 5 don't make their own programmes, they commission them from independent production companies. This means that there are opportunities to work in the commissioning departments for both channels. Basically, you become a temp and then see if you can wangle your way to a more permanent position (which is a regular occurrence).

Breaking into the biz can be done, no matter who you are or where you come from. All your experience and contacts will enrich your life and help you achieve your writing goals.

I got work at Channel 4 through a temp agency. All you have to do is phone up the personnel department of a channel, ask what temp agencies they use and then go from there. This temp job at Channel 4 was for two weeks but in the end I stayed for four years, working my way into a full-time position in the comedy department. I got to know all about Channel 4, the programmes it made, the people responsible for them and how the commissioning process worked. I loved every minute.

GET A WRITING JOB IN TV

If you're keen to make it as a TV writer, then an inevitable step in the process is to write a trial episode for one of the soaps. These trials are also known as shadow schemes. Essentially, you'll go through the process of writing a real episode from the official storylines without it actually being broadcast. There usually isn't a fee for trial episodes, although some of the one-hour dramas may offer some remuneration.

A trial episode is a big deal. It's make or break time. In some instances, you'll be asked to write a handful of sample scenes to see if you're suitable to write an entire trial episode. Other times, the sample scenes will be enough to guarantee a commission. It varies from show to show. Let's break it down.

Sample scenes

"Sample scenes" may sound fairly straightforward, but you'll probably be asked to write 10–15 scenes, or maybe even half an episode. This will usually be the A story of the intended episode, to see how you get on with the characters, dialogue and the arc of that particular plot line.

Trial episode

This process includes a first draft, notes from the script editor, then a second draft before a decision is made on whether or not you're suited to the show. Naturally, writing the entire episode gives a much fuller indication of how well you know the series, the characters, etc. It's also a lot harder than you think. You might be good enough to write for the show, but there's a lot of competition. You won't be the only one doing a trial episode. Make your script shine.

Approach

Some soaps use scene-by-scene breakdowns (written by the storyliners), and you write the script from there. Others give you a two- or three-page outline of what happens in your episode, and it's up to you to come up with the scenes, structure, etc. Whatever the case, you may settle down to write, telling yourself not to stray too much from what you've been given, and to give them what they want.

This is a bad approach. As it's a trial, they want to see your take on the episode, your original voice. This means giving them what they want, but not necessarily what they expect.

Work out the stories. What's really going on? Is there a better beat to be had? What's the character feeling? Is my B story really the A story? Follow the flow of what you need to do, but don't just hit the beats. Add flavour, humour, surprise, something that says "YOU" but within the acceptable context of the show.

When you're familiar with a series, then follow your instincts on how the characters would react and behave. When you're unfamiliar, you probably just want the writing gig and your lack of passion or awareness will show.

If you want to break away from some of the storyline, don't be afraid to speak to the script editor and discuss your thoughts. Give solid reasoning for why a character would or wouldn't do something. Script editors will know more than you in terms of the wider impact of what you're suggesting, so if they agree with you, you're on the right track. If they think you should stick to the storyline, then listen to what they have to say.

Notes

It's important, nay vital, to take on notes; but it's equally important not to slavishly follow what you've been told (especially if you disagree or don't understand). Absorb the notes as much as possible so you understand the underlying emotions and motivations of what you're being asked to do. That way, you can remain creative in your dramatisation (sometimes surprising the script editor) but still stick to the overall sense of what they want. Avoid using the script editor's suggestions verbatim. Notes are guidelines and suggestions, not instructions or demands. They can be very specific at times, but there's usually a good reason. It's a tricky balance.

Handle with care. If in doubt, *speak to your script editor.*

Characters

The most common form of rejection when writing trial episodes is "we felt you didn't suitably know the characters". While you may think you've done what you've been told and followed the storyline, it may read quite bland or safe. You haven't given the characters some personal sense of detail, dialogue, humour or an unexpected (but plausible) turn of behaviour. The most important part of any trial episode is to *know the characters.* Know how they speak and behave, and what personal history/relationship can be interwoven into the storyline.

Tip

Watch the show with the subtitles on. Get familiar with the rhythm, tone and tempo of how various characters talk. Soap dialogue can be very tight and sparse, but the subtitles occasionally trim the lines back further. Watch and learn.

Overview

TV writing is hard work. There's a lot to consider, not to mention understanding the production documents that detail what sets or actors are available, and other restrictions. But this is the process, this is the reality. Do your research. Immerse yourself in the show as much as possible. Be prepared, and then impress them with your love of the show and how your original voice will add to the continued success of the series.

> *They want you to bring your own voice, but without 'breaking' the show.*

James Moran

KIDS' TV

Writing for kids' television is challenging, fun, and profitable. It also requires the same amount of screenwriting skill and craft as writing any other drama. It can actually be much harder because you'll often be expected to write a funny script. No postmodern cultural references, intellectual quips or self-reflective wit, just make the script funny through the characters and story. No pressure.

Writing for kids is the purest form of storytelling because it's free of ego and cynicism. Kids don't care if you're Russell T Davies. They only care if Russell T Davies tells them a good story. An idea that grabs. A story with a sense of urgency. Characters who we really care about. A plot with unpredictable twists and turns. Think kids aren't sophisticated and can't see a twist from a mile away? Think again.

Kids' TV breaks down into a number of different categories: drama, factual, animation, light entertainment and pre-school. Pre-school targets 0–4-year-olds: colourful worlds and characters specific to positive child development (e.g. *Teletubbies*). Drama and animation for 4–12-year-olds are broken down into sub-categories of target age groups: 4–6, 6–9 and 9–12-year-olds. 6–9-year-olds is the sweet spot for most kids' TV. Shows targeted at 9–12-year-olds will typically be more ambitious and adventure-led, like *The Sarah Jane Adventures* and *Leonardo*.

How do you get the opportunity to write for kids' TV? Well, it's the same process as primetime drama or feature films. You need to have written a spec script, and preferably a spec script in the kids' TV genre. Formats for kids' TV tend to be shorter (e.g. 11-minute episodes), so a 15-page spec script would suffice (especially if it's backed up with a series bible that expands the characters and world of the story). Then you target the relevant producers and production companies that are making kids' TV shows.

If your query/approach lands at the right time and place, you may very well find yourself pitching for a commission. Pitching for a commission means that the producers are willing to receive ideas from you as potential episodes of their show. You don't (typically) get paid for this. The pitches are usually a paragraph long, a page at most. If the idea is accepted, then you'll be commissioned to script, with the usual outline and scene-by-scene stages in between. Occasionally, you may be invited to "writer workshops" (and receive a modest attendance fee) where a number of writers will meet to discuss the series (the tone, characters, rules, etc.), and after that, you'll be asked to submit ideas. But just because you've attended the workshop, there's no guarantee of a commission unless the idea is really good.

When Danny first started writing for kids' TV, he quickly discovered that he loved working in the genre, but that it was just as hard as some of his primetime TV/film work. Each kids' show he's worked on has been a specific challenge in terms of its style of humour and storytelling, from the visual gags of *The Amazing Adrenalini Brothers*, to the teen hang-ups in *Sofia's*

Diary, the live-action/animation mock-doc combo of *Roy*, and the gross-out antics of *Fleabag Monkeyface*, not to mention the sophisticated adventures of *Octonauts* and *Thunderbirds Are Go!*

The number one rule when writing for kids' TV is: Never be patronising to your audience. Kids are far smarter than their parents, especially when it comes to story! Another good consideration is that stories should be child*like* rather than child*ish*. Childlike means having that sense of fun, curiosity and optimism about the world. Childish antics have their place (as many characters might have a childish outlook) but silly and stupid behaviour just for the sake of it doesn't do anybody any favours.

Over on Twitter, Danny asked some lovely TV folk to share their tips and advice on writing for kids' TV. A lot of their answers chimed with the above, but here's a selection of replies.

Phil Ford, writer of *The Sarah Jane Adventures* and *Wizards Vs Aliens* (with Russell T Davies):

> *If you think of a story you don't think you could write for kids, write it! The best kids' TV challenges its audience, and most of all challenges the writer. Writing good kids' TV is tough work!*

Debbie Moon, BAFTA-winning writer of *Wolfblood* for CBBC:

> *Remember you're writing for a broad age range. Kids' TV is often defined as 8–12s but there could be much younger siblings in the room. Kids have specific concerns: family, friendship, loyalty, fitting in. Boyfriend/girlfriend relationships not a big concern. Oh, and you can't kill human beings. Aliens are OK but no humans (one of the few drawbacks to writing for kids!).*

James Henry (*Bob the Builder, Hey Duggee*):

> *If it's the pre-school demographic, try not to give any character dialogue that runs for more than two lines. Try to have problems solved with a nice visual/action rather than characters just talking to each other.*

Yvonne Grace (*My Dad's a Boring Nerd*):

> *NEVER underestimate kids' ability to catch on and interpret complex ideas.*

Mark Huckerby and Nick Ostler, Emmy-nominated writers, *Peter Rabbit*:

> *Kids' shows eat up stories. 52 eps not unusual. Schedules are brutal. Be head writer's friend by being a problem solver... take notes well, they might seem silly but there's usually a good reason for them, write fast, but don't be sloppy... be prolific with ideas, but be prepared to dig deep for original ones, don't submit first thoughts, they'll be clichés. Don't assume because it's for kids that the storytelling standards should be any lower!*

PRIMETIME DRAMA

> " *If you're working on a TV show in production there isn't a lot of time to faff around. We're filming in three months, we need an outline now. You need to find the answers immediately.* "
>
> James Moran

Working as a regular writer on TV soaps will usually give you enough street cred (or "flying hours" as Kate Harwood, former BBC Production Head of Drama, likes to call it) to tackle the bigger scale and kudos of primetime TV.

This means stepping up from the half-hour format to the more meaty and challenging world of 60-minute dramas, comedy dramas, or crime/medical shows. It's rare for an unknown writer or a writer without any previous experience to be commissioned to write a 60-minute script. When it does occur, it's usually with good reason: the writer is an award-winning playwright, or someone the producer knows or trusts despite their lack of flying hours (and they'll help them through the process).

REMEMBER
Think about the other side

If you don't want to write for the soaps yet want to write your own primetime series (or work for an existing series), then you're going to have to earn the right to do so. Maybe you've made a low-budget film that's done well on the indie circuit, winning an award or two or gaining critical acclaim; that would help to bypass the soap route and go straight to the top of the primetime "consider" list. Similarly, an award-winning play, even a short film (BAFTA or Oscar award-winning, preferably) would probably ensure at least a meeting with the TV big bods.

But don't be hasty, and don't be snobby. There's lots of good work and great writing in the soaps. Dive in, dig in, learn your craft, earn some money, get better as a writer, and then you'll be more experienced and ready to tackle the primetime opportunities that will come your way.

MINI-SERIES

It's worth noting that mini-series are author-led and so will usually have a well-known or established writer to drive the heart of the narrative. Mini-series are often about social, political and topical issues, and/or will have an "event" feel to them.

Also, the closed nature of the story (i.e. it has a definite resolution) is what gives them their mini-series status, rather than the premise/characters being a launchpad for an ongoing series.

While it's a good idea to have a mini-series treatment or script as part of a wider slate, we would not recommend trying to "jump in" with a mini-series as a new writer, or have unrealistic expectations of getting it off the ground.

> *Innovation is a must. We should be giving the audience not what they want, but what they never dreamed of. Offering a surprise, delivering characters that are really real – that's what we must do. Surprise and real characters have become the territory of reality TV. But that's our job! That's what we should be doing! We must be the most exciting thing in the room. Are we being bold enough?*

Barbara Machin
TV Writer
Waking the Dead, Casualty

Mini-Series Examples:

- *State of Play* by Paul Abbott
- *Red Riding* and *Southcliffe* by Tony Grisoni
- *Our Friends in the North* by Peter Flannery
- *Dead Set* by Charlie Brooker (also *Black Mirror*, to some extent)
- *The Singing Detective* by Dennis Potter

GET A JOB IN FILM

There are a number of opportunities in and avenues towards TV that will get you the kick-start and contacts you need for your career. Do the same exist for film?

Well, yes and no.

It's probably fair to say that the world of film is much more of a closed shop than TV. But that doesn't mean that the shop is entirely closed to you. You can be canny enough to figure out its opening times and raid the store for everything they've got.

REMEMBER
There is
no 'inside'

To get by in this world it's often who you know rather than what you know that will determine your fate. But what is not added to this adage is that, while someone you know might get you the opportunity, it's down to your talent and hard work to ensure that the nepotism or favouritism is justified. Otherwise, in the immortal words of *The Apprentice*, "you're fired".

The notion of "six degrees of separation" should probably read "three degrees of separation". You'd be surprised how you can link yourself to someone who has some tie to the industry and who might, just might, be able to swing something your way.

Your cousin's wife's sister could work for a post-production house and might be prepared to have a word with her boss about the possibility of getting you in as a runner, or in dispatch, or just sitting in on some edits and learning a few things.

Some people, especially those new and naïve to the business, go to the Cineplex and check out what's on offer and think there's no way of breaking into that world. But that's high-profile cinema. The top-end of production and distribution. You can't just walk into that arena without earning your stripes first.

There are lots of films being made, every day. These include shorts, low- or no-budget features, pop promos, commercials and corporate videos. And while they generally crew up quite quickly, there's still that small gap of uncertainty for a production manager when they have to consider: "Who can I get as a runner? What about a production secretary?"

When we were crewing up our own low-budget feature (*Who Killed Nelson Nutmeg?*), we were pleased to get emails from runners who offered something different and interesting – whether that was their location, knowledge of the genre or technical specialism. Obviously, those who sent a generic email with no indication that they'd checked out our project went to the bottom of the pile.

This is where you come in. Your unbridled passion and enthusiasm will have generated some momentum where you'll find yourself in a position of contact for producers or execs.

What's out there? You know it already. Despite the occasional weary criticism from its own members, Shooting People is recruiting practically every day for films, shorts and scripts. It may be payment on a low deferment basis but remember, everyone's got to start somewhere. There are also ever-changing Facebook and LinkedIn groups that do the same.

Screen International is the film industry trade mag for the UK and will sometimes slip in an advert for development staff.

You could try the reliable approach of writing to film companies with your CV. As a lot of people do this, it really has to be a good letter, practically a winning pitch of yourself, for it to work. Although, if you're wily and witty enough, follow it up with a phone call (see previous section on TV) and see how far you can get. Especially if you have a unique angle, as the people who contacted us for our film did.

Working Title Films have an annual (open) internship called Action. Check their website for details. "The successful candidates will spend 12 months with Working Title on a full-time basis with the development and production teams." This is an amazing opportunity. Make sure you're first in line. Annihilate the opposition with your commitment to film.

Don't be afraid to use your contacts or any industry relatives you might (tenuously) have. Danny's mother's cousin worked in special effects in Ardmore Studios and lo, his first break in film was born. But through his own hustle, Danny got a job doing film reviews on RTÉ all because he used the right approach. Then he moved to London and got a two-week temp job in Channel 4 that lasted for four years.

CLASSIC OPPORTUNITIES

The main thrust of a career

1 – Competitions

Get involved and enter those that will work for you and your scripts.

2 – Apply for jobs

Think about joining the industry as a way of getting on the ladder.

3 – Know how writers start in TV

Hone your skills in writing episodes for long-running shows and check out shadow schemes.

4 – Don't forget about film

If you want to gain experience, then remember people are always shooting low-budget short films.

MAINSTREAM **O**PPORTUNITIES

These opportunities for writers are, perhaps, just outside of what you want to do long term. But, in the meantime, they can be a handy source of income that is related to writing, while still ensuring that you're building good contacts for the future. You may do one of these opportunities, several, or none.

> *Get a backup career. If you want to tell your own stories in your own way then it's a hard life. So you probably need to do something else. That something else should be film-related, but another source of cash. I've been a film critic for example.*

John Waters
Filmmaking legend

SCRIPT READING

The role of script reader is a thankless and anonymous one, but every production company will tell you that readers are vital to wading through the submission pile and the development process.

Producers and development execs simply don't have the time to read every script that comes in the door, and they rely squarely on the reader's report and recommendation.

Readers are usually involved in the industry in another similar role, such as script editor or writer, so they have a full and frank appreciation of what a screenplay should epitomise.

To be a reputable script reader, it takes more than attending a course about "how to read a script", and a bit more dedication than reading for a few weeks just to get the hang of it and make a few contacts. Readers new to the process complain that it takes up too much time and it pays too little (roughly about four hours' work @ £40 a script). Others moan that they've read too much that week but the scripts still keep on coming.

Well, it does take up time and it doesn't pay a wage, but the execs have a never-ending spec pile that needs to get covered, so the work has to be done regardless of who does it. They don't care as long as the script gets read, but they'll always lean on the more reliable readers rather than someone who's let them down in the past.

But how do you get this work?

How can you find the lucky break to become a script reader in the first place?

Unfortunately, there are no short cuts or easy routes. Script reading is never advertised. It comes about solely through word-of-mouth recommendations and whatever contacts you can hustle into giving you a go. Cold calling may be a frustrating and fruitless task but it's still worth a shot. The main thing to remember is to make a strong approach – polite, passionate and professional – as this will help you to stand out from the crowd.

The leading production companies get several requests per week from people wanting to script read for them. Invariably, these requests will get politely declined. However, if you have a recommendation from someone, or can name-drop someone the exec might know, this could help to get you in the door. Ideally, you should have a sample report ready that demonstrates you're capable of doing the job, or the exec might assign a trial report (unpaid) to see what you're like (as they may not be familiar with the script from your own sample report).

Execs and producers want people who know how to read a script and, more importantly, they like readers who can articulate a synopsis with insightful comments to match. They don't want glib, dismissive, cynical or superficial reports that bring more attention to the reader than the script they're covering. It's all about the script, and whether the writer is worth a mention. The reader remains thankless, anonymous, and goes on to the next script.

The best advice to someone who wants to be a reader and has no prior experience is to approach agents and/or production companies, and offer to read their scripts free for two weeks. This will give you enough time to gather a range of sample script reports. After that, the production companies may pay you to continue reading for them, and if they don't, you'll be able to approach other companies with your sample reports in hand.

But if you're thinking it'll be a cool gig for a week or a month or two, then you're better off trawling through Drew's Script-O-Rama for the research you're after. As a regular reader, you'll find yourself unwittingly sucked into the routine of dropping off scripts/picking them up. It will seem never-ending, it will sometimes feel not worth it, but for those dedicated to the craft of screenwriting, there'll be no other option than to continue to read the good, the bad and the ugly. Authors read books, musicians read music, scriptwriters and script editors should read scripts, wherever they can find them.

Scripts, in the industry, are seen as bait to get actors.

Iain Softley
Director

WRITING A SCRIPT REPORT

Like any good writing document, a script report has a basic structure that is convenient to adhere to. Sometimes, after reading a script, the reader can think: "Crikey, what am I going to say about that?" But this is where the basic structure of a report is a valuable tool of reference. Below are some useful headings that help focus your thoughts and could be used to break up your report into sensible paragraphs. They also highlight how your script will be broken down in assessment by the industry.

Concept

First, talk about the concept: is the idea any good? Is it commercially appealing or more intellectual and discerning? Is it just a shameless rip-off of a million genre flicks before it? Or does it bring something new to the table? Is it genre?

Plot

Does it make sense? Is it convincing and/or original? Too predictable maybe? Jumbled?

Structure

Is there a basic understanding of craft on display? Is it a join-the-dots three-act structure, or does it contain a solid and reliable framework to tell its story? However, the reader shouldn't get bogged down in restructuring tips because it's not a script editing exercise.

Characters

Are the central and minor characters believable, original, compelling, inspiring, colourful, loathsome, boring, etc? Decent character development or emotional journey for the protagonist? Effective use of subplot with the supporting characters?

Dialogue

Distinctive, realistic, off-the-wall, on-the-nose, funny, dull, plain, quirky, true to each character?

Tone

Does the writer have an original voice? Is the tone of the story consistent to the genre, etc?

Pace

Pace, rhythm, tempo. Scenes start too soon, too late? Cut too soon, too late? Boring segments with little dramatic impact or importance? Where does the pace flag? What's its overall effectiveness?

Setting

Is it important to the story – does it make a valid and visual contribution to the characters and plot? Is it noteworthy at all?

Appeal

Will the idea and story find an audience? Who is the audience? Is it marketable? Is it really cinematic?

And to quote direct advice from one particular report format (although it generally applies to all):

> The bottom line is, does the piece have real potential or not? If it reminds you of any other film, feel free to compare it, that can be really useful, and if there are elements attached, particularly a director, do take note of that in your report. If you're convinced it's a pass, give us something positive to say to the producer or writer either in person or in a letter as well as a good reason to pass on it. Try to put yourself in our shoes and imagine you were telling someone kindly why you don't want to pursue the project. Don't make the mistake of being casual or dismissive however you might personally feel about the writing, as we're looking for a professional and

objective appraisal, and not flippant comments however amusing. Finally, please make it as readable as possible – remember that we read tons of these reports a week.

SCRIPT EDITING

Some script readers become script editors. A script editor helps the writer over several drafts to refine and improve the screenplay.

Their goal is to help the writer get the best possible script that will meet the needs of those who want it.

A writer may hire a script editor to help them get their spec script into great shape to approach producers. Or a production company may give a scriptwriter a script editor.

Andrew Ellard is a well-known script editor, having worked on *The IT Crowd*, *Red Dwarf*, *Miranda* and *Count Arthur Strong*. On his (great) Twitter feed, he boiled down the role of a script editor into three types: Conduit, Contributor and Consultant. He explains:

"**Conduit:** Runs many writers. Collates notes from above. Tracks drafts/details. Organise-y & admin-y. Big with soaps.

Contributor: A writer by another name. Providing material more than analysis - gags and ideas. Big on comedies.

Consultant: Story & character analysis - pre and post drafts. Detailed notes. Works directly with writer-showrunners. My gig.

To be clear: those #scripteditors roles are the boiled-down basics. In the wild it's inevitable that there's crossover between them.

Point is: Script Editor means many different things. The same title on *The Bill* and *Peep Show* can mean wildly different jobs."

We highly recommend you follow Andrew on Twitter for regular insights, especially his **#tweetnotes** https://twitter.com/ellardent

WRITING FOR RADIO

Many UK writers and comedians make their name on radio before they make that all-important transition to television, the theatre or even the big screen. It's a route that is not often considered by new writers but should be given some serious thought because of the many opportunities that exist within the format.

In the UK, BBC radio drama is the place to go if you want to get one of your plays on air. BBC Radio 4 has the majority of slots: the afternoon play, the Friday play, the Saturday play, classic serial, *Woman's Hour* drama, afternoon reading, *Book at Bedtime*, *Book of the Week* and, of course, *The Archers*. On Radio 3 there's the Sunday play at 8pm, as well as *The Wire,* which aims to push the boundaries of drama using first-time writers.

That's a lot of slots. A lot of plays. A lot of writers. A lot of opportunities. How do you get your idea commissioned? At the time of press, the BBC split the year into two commissioning rounds, one in March/April, the other in September/October. They accept and develop ideas during these periods to give themselves enough plays to cover their demanding schedule throughout the year. However, it is extremely difficult to get an idea approved as a writer alone. It is preferable, nay essential, that you attach yourself to either an in-house producer or an independent production company that specialises in radio plays. That way your idea has more clout and more chance of actually getting commissioned.

The radio process is similar to the stage in that it completely respects the writer during the development and production of the play. Not a word changes without the writer's permission! Maybe it's time to start tuning in, and get inspired to write a radio play.

Make sure to bookmark BBC's radio commissioning pages to stay right up to date:

http://www.bbc.co.uk/commissioning/radio/

http://www.bbc.co.uk/commissioning/radio/what-we-want/radio-4.shtml

WRITING FOR THEATRE

We are continually told that execs are looking for writers who have an original voice or have something interesting to say. The spec screenplay pile doesn't offer a lot of distinctive voices or innovative material. A lot of the time, execs will turn to the theatre to see which writers are making their mark.

It's not a huge leap from theatre to screenwriting, and a lot of successful writers have learned their craft by dabbling with more experimental fare on radio and the stage. But we don't know a great deal about it. Luckily, **Tom Green** does (http://www.tomgreen-uk.com/).. Here, he shares his insights into writing for theatre:

"The basics

As with any form of dramatic writing, there are no limits to subject or scale. But more theatres will be able to stage a two-person show than one with a cast of thirty.

People in theatre seem less hung up about structure than their film and TV equivalents but the same "rules" still apply – after all, Aristotle wasn't writing about feature films. On the whole, risk-taking in both form and content is encouraged. If you can tell a good story and create controversy then you're made.

For some basic "how-to" advice try *Playwriting 101* by Jon Dorf. *The Playwriting Seminars* by Richard Toscan is also useful, even though it's very badly designed.

There is no single set format for play manuscripts, just make a clear distinction between dialogue and action and make it clear who is speaking.

What's in it for you?

You're unlikely to get rich writing plays. Even if you do manage to get something staged at a decent venue you won't be giving up the day job any time soon. A writer told me recently that she'd made more from a single episode of *Hollyoaks* that she wrote in three weeks than from a commissioned play that took her two years.

The benefits come primarily from the working process – writers tend to be more involved, and listened to, than they might be in film or TV. And seeing your work performed in front of an audience is invaluable.

You'll also find that, if you can get something produced, people in TV, as well as theatre, will take notice. If you get some good reviews, expect to find agents knocking on your door.

Getting staged

There are only a handful of new writing theatres, but most of them will (eventually) read what you send them and, if they like it, they'll try to find a way to get you involved in a writing group or scheme. Don't expect it to be any easier than getting into TV or film, though.

While getting a play on at a mainstream theatre is the goal, you can also try the fringe. It's not cheap – perhaps £150 plus per night to hire the venue, for starters – but if you can raise the money it's a way to get your work seen and your name known.

Some new writing theatres in London:

* The Royal Court
* Soho Theatre
* Hampstead Theatre
* The Bush Theatre
* Paines Plough
* Theatre Royal, Stratford East

 A useful list of London fringe venues at http://www.OffWestEnd.com

Outside London:

* Liverpool Everyman
* Liverpool's New Writing Theatre
* The Traverse, Edinburgh
* Edinburgh Fringe
* The Royal Exchange Theatre, Manchester

If you are interested in writing for the theatre, the best (and most obvious) thing to do first is read a lot of plays and go to the theatre as much as possible."

CORPORATES

As we all know, even the biggest writers and directors often do paid gigs as a writer for hire. It's a chance to fund personal projects or get some income to give precious development time. Yet the skills needed for this kind of work are not very often discussed. It's perhaps assumed that as it's "lower" than TV writing, it's simpler. But it actually has its own formats to be aware of and specific techniques that need to be mastered.

One thing to note is that this can be a profitable venture where you get paid a good day rate, often between £200 and £350. The downside is that the deadlines will be tight.

There are so many formats you can use for these ideas – drama clips, interviews, talking heads, interactive activities, etc. This can be daunting if you're used to only writing TV-style drama. You have to open up your mind slightly to think about all the different styles of moving image.

Whatever format you use, the one rule we would recommend observing when delivering to the brief is this:

Your script should allow the audience to understand the message that needs to be communicated in a simple way – and in a way that they want.

But what does that mean? We once wrote the video sections for an online learning course around staying safe during international business travel – avoiding using dodgy taxis, not getting pickpocketed, staying away from scams. You get the idea.

One way to do this would be to have a presenter telling the viewer all about it. Fine, the content would be covered. But that approach doesn't really mirror the event as the viewer would experience it in real life. That may leave holes in their knowledge.

For this project we did things like shoot a two-minute

point-of-view scene – walking out of a hotel, encountering a number of characters. The viewer had to rate them on screen depending on how risky they felt the situation was.

This way, the viewer lived the experience as they learned. Therefore, if they face a similar situation in the future, they'll know what to do.

Getting corporate work

If you have a previous working life, use that as a jumping-in point. Let's say you used to work in the NHS: you will be ideally placed to write scripts for trusts, the Care Quality Commission, medical suppliers and so on. You know the lingo *and* you can write. How would you land a gig like this?

Think about what potential customers/clients want. For example:

- make more sales
- train people to be better at their jobs
- bring in investment
- keep customers informed of changes
- engage staff.

No one in the corporate world wants to "buy a script". What happens is they realise they need a video to help them achieve their goals.

Approaching companies as an individual writer offering these types of scripts/videos isn't ideal. However, you, alongside a production company, might have some powerful ideas to help a client reach twice as many customers for less money, and that's a fantastic approach.

Find corporate production companies and explain to them how your writing will help their productions. Use an internet search to identify local companies or companies that concentrate on your business/specialised area.

COMPUTER AND VIDEO GAMES

Writing content for video games differs a lot from writing screenplays and we will look at the differences (as well as the similarities) here.

Before that, here are five things you may be unaware of with regards to writing for games.

1 – Size of the industry

The games industry is worth $45billion worldwide – so

there is money around. The UK is still a player (just about), so you can get a foot in the door. A big UK multiplayer online game will cost £50m to develop. Compare that to how many UK £50m films there are.

2 – It's not for kids

The average age of players is now 33. Your game writing doesn't have to be childish stuff – unless you want it to be.

3 – Games aren't for gamers

Not a hard-core full-on nerdy gamer? Well, that's cool. Neither are the majority of people who play games. They play on their Wii, or their iPhone, and they play with friends.

4 – You don't have to sit on your own

The biggest games right now are Facebook games and online games. The lonely teenage gamer in his bedroom is now rare.

5 – The script is a small part, you need to let go

When you have actors on a stage, the director sets the rules and the script is their guide. In games it's the same thing, but one step further removed. The game sets up the rules and we're all actors on the stage. The script is a guide for us all. Games have become much more complex and character-led. But they've also become much less on-rails and more open world.

Skills

You're not expected to have any programming or coding skills. Your job is about crafting words. But what skills are needed and do you have them?

Transferable skills

Storytelling: Generally saying interesting things, using your imagination to conceive of intriguing situations – that will always be the key skill. It's easy to forget that other people really struggle with this, so pack your suitcase full of cool stuff.

Wide range of influences: Writers are good at drawing in ideas from everywhere. Other people in the games industry sometimes get stuck in a certain genre or a way of working. They may repeat ideas or remain on a familiar set of tracks. Bringing in ideas from outside the genre is welcomed.

Rewriting and then rewriting again: someone who

doesn't mind going back through work for repeated drafts will be met with open arms. Pressure on a project can come from hardware restrictions, coding issues, graphics constraints, all sorts of directions – you may need to keep reworking your drafts through no fault of your own. And not moan about it. We can all tick that one off.

Dialogue: We've all played games where the dialogue is awful – of a sub-TV movie quality. That's because someone in the company did it who shouldn't have. Obviously, if you're hired it's because at least someone has recognised their weakness in this area. All your usual dialogue skill and techniques will work here: people not saying exactly what they mean, using dialects, adding personal quirks, etc.

Curiosity: Again, an undervalued skill as we take it for granted. Why would someone do that? What kind of person says that? If I was like that, what would I do?

Think of the audience: Or in this case, the player. Will people be able to follow the game? How many plots and characters can any one person follow?

Different skills you will now need

New structures: All the theories about three-act, nine-act or sequence structure don't really matter at all anymore. The structure will be set by the gameplay mechanics and you have to fit within that. As an example, the game may be mission-based. If a mission lasts x minutes then that's how long it lasts. Fit around it. Remember, you do the same in film where you work around the length of an old film reel – it's just the technology has moved on since then and the structural ideas haven't.

Living with the vague: In a film, as you know, there's all sorts of fun to be had by playing around with what the characters know, and what the audience knows that the characters don't know. But if you're doing a non-linear game, that's all jettisoned. You don't know what the player knows. This may take some time to get used to.

Technical nous: If you're the kind of writer who struggles with Final Draft software and sending an email, this may not be the right job for you. You'll need to get into a bit of techie stuff just to make sure your work comes out OK. Being able to find your way around servers is a prerequisite of the job.

Grammar: Some of your work will be text-based as well as dialogue-based, so brush up on your grammar and spelling.

Style of interaction: You'll be collaborating closely with others rather than being an isolated writer. Even if you are a collaborating kind of writer, the style of working together may be different. Table readings are out. Playtests are in – followed by discussion on a wiki. Everyone uses instant messenger. Even people who are 10 feet away!

Industry awareness: A small shift in behaviour, this. Few want to talk about *12 Years A Slave*, but they can pull apart why *Uncharted 3* works. TV is out. iPlayer is in.

How to apply

1 – Know where to look

The writing-style jobs will normally be in the "design" section of a website. Design means the games content. Design doesn't mean visual or graphic design: that's called "art". Sometimes the writing jobs appear in "audio" if the work is writing spoken dialogue. Hunt around. And as all of this suggests – yes, these opportunities are actually advertised openly!

2 – Know your job terms

This is a potential nightmare. Not all jobs for writers include the term "writer" or "scriptwriter". In film and TV we have more than our fair share of crazy job titles (Best Boy, etc.), but at least these are standard across the biz. There is no such uniformity or consistency in games. Tim's official title working on one game was

Senior Creative Designer, and yet he did the writing. Explore deeper into the jobs and read the descriptions.

3 – Know how to approach a company

Whether it's through an agency, a website, or a speculative approach, the advice is the same. In fact, it's the same for *any* writing job. Stress your skills that are an exact match. Mention your skills that are transferable and don't be afraid to join the dots – "I can do *x* which will help you do *y*". But best of all, get some relevant experience in the following areas (in descending order):

i) big-budget games

ii) freeware games, including mods or flash games

iii) interactive products – CD-ROMs, large websites with entertaining content, non-linear narratives

iv) other involvement in the games industry – for example, Tim was on the BAFTA games-judging panel a couple of times

v) basic game play – know how games work, in detail

vi) passion for gaming

Success in other fields of writing (comics, TV, films, novels) helps also.

If you're not a fan of games, then you probably shouldn't waste everyone's time by applying. That would be the same as turning up for a potential gig on *EastEnders* and admitting you don't like TV.

COPYWRITING/ADVERTISING

"Story" is big in marketing these days. But does that mean there are opportunities for writers in this field? It does.

Tim John, author of *Adventures in LA-LA Land* (about his journey to being a Hollywood writer), started out in the advertising business, promoting products such as Findus Crispy Pancakes!

This kind of role only suits certain writers – it requires a lot of brainstorming and the ability to formulate very short and powerful phrases.

You're writing to a brief, and often quite a tight one. But the financial rewards may outweigh the challenge.

Perhaps the only slight negative around this opportunity is the fact that there are now specialist courses in this field, meaning you may be competing against people of a similar level of experience, but with much more training.

MAINSTREAM OPPORTUNITIES

Some ideas to expand your career

1 – Script reading

Get better at writing by reading, and also build your industry knowledge and contacts.

2 – Radio

A sideways route into larger broadcasters.

3 – Theatre

Great for stories with minimal characters.

4 – Corporate

Lacking in glamour perhaps, but regular work that pays well, if you make the right kind of approach.

5 – Games

A big industry that openly advertises positions.

6 – Copywriting/Advertising

There are opportunities here, if brevity is your thing!

NICHE OPPORTUNITIES

Sometimes it's better to look at smaller or niche markets for your writing. These opportunities are more unusual and won't suit all writers. But they may suit you!

REMEMBER
Do it your way, today

> *It's a crowded market, very crowded. So be bold, go for broke, make a noise. If you fail then people will at least think you are mad – and as a madman you'll get more room on the sidewalk.*

Guy Maddin
Writer and Director
Winner of the Telluride Lifetime Achievement Award

WEB SERIES

Writing for a web series can be a great opportunity, if very low paid. There's usually not much money to be made as most revenue is ad-based and the majority of web series don't pull in big audiences.

However, many are being made all the time, the production time is fast and the episodes are short – meaning you can churn them out. Maybe you even fancy getting involved in producing your own, too.

Here are **7 simple ideas to consider when creating a web series.**

1 – Be close

The audience and the writer/web series makers must be as close as possible. One of the main benefits of working on a web series is that there aren't people like executives or distributors getting in the way – but the key is to make the effort to connect with your audience via social media.

2 – Making it together

Give the audience room to engage. Not to drive the plot: that's your job. But to steer the overall direction. What elements ignite their interest? Should episodes be shorter? Listen to audience feedback/reaction.

3 – Honesty

No one has all the answers to how to make a perfect web series. Don't pretend otherwise. Overcoming obstacles is more interesting than just appearing to magically get it right. Audiences sometimes don't mind if something is rough around the edges, it can add to the charm!

4 – Make it worth talking about

Word of mouth can sometimes be the enemy of traditional movies. Poor word of mouth fights against their blanket marketing technique. A web series relies on word of mouth (or word of mouse) to spread. Make your film worth talking about.

5 – A story lasts forever

Therefore invest in the story. The rest of the production may be low budget, but the story should never feel low grade.

6 – "A film for..." NOT "A film by..."

No one cares who you are. But they care if you made a story for people like them.

7 – No snobbery

It doesn't matter how people see the web series – phone, big screen, download. It only matters that they see it. Also, most people don't care what it was shot on. Get over any snobbery and just try to deliver a story that people will enjoy and want to share with friends. That's a big challenge!

COMICS

We haven't done much comic book writing, but when we did it was with **Mike Garley**. Here's a special guest section from him:

"Comics are a unique visual medium that allow writers to tell stories unrestricted by budget, location, and actors' availability, and perhaps even more unique to the medium, comics aren't restricted to a set publishing or distribution method.

The majority of comic creators start out by telling their own, original stories and either paying collaborators (artists, colourists, letterers, etc.) to work with them, or offering a share, where profits are split once/if a project starts to earn.

If you're thinking of pitching your comic, then you'll be

able to find a list of what publishers are looking for on their websites, which you can, and should, refer to before starting down that route. Getting published is no easy task, with lots of competition; you'll need to make sure that your pitch really stands out, and to be prepared for a potentially long wait before seeing your comic reach print.

Another avenue open to you is self-publishing where you can either finance a print run yourself, or look for crowdfunding with the likes of Kickstarter and Indiegogo. The majority of creators start out like this as it's a fantastic way of learning on the job as well as proving that you're not afraid to put your money where your mouth is.

REMEMBER
Do it your
way, today

Once you have a comic or two (although I think a more realistic number is twelve) under your belt, then you can start to approach publishers about licensed characters. Editors will need to see your ability to tell a story in a sequential format, and there's no better way to get the attention of an editor than by handing them a sample of your work.

Comics are notoriously low paying, but they do allow you the ability to create vast and unique worlds, and assemble a body of work. Comics are big business at the moment and producers are actively searching for the next big thing. That doesn't mean that it's easy, because it's not. Comics are hard, but you get to work in an incredibly creative industry and produce unique stories that can be as visually and narratively distinctive as you like!"

Read more about Mike Garley's work
http://mikegarley.com

INTERACTIVE FICTION AND TRANSMEDIA

This whole topic may strike fear (or confusion) into writers. This survival handbook is all about helping writers earn a living by looking for new ways to find work and new opportunities. There is probably no newer opportunity than transmedia.

So what is it exactly?

Well, it's so new that there's no fixed answer to that

question yet. Another name for transmedia storytelling is multiplatform narrative. This is perhaps easier to understand. It's a story that spans formats or media. A common mistake is to get that mixed up with cross-platform adaptations.

Let's look at the difference with an example: if you watch Christopher Nolan's *The Dark Knight*, then read the novelisation, then read the comic book adaptation, that isn't a transmedia experience. You have read the same story, but in three different media.

The current Marvel universe is more of a transmedia experience. You watch the films. Then the TV spin-offs. Then you can play a game where you control one of the minor characters from the film during a new adventure that overlaps with the film. This is more transmedia in nature in that to get the whole story you use different media.

Of course, a good transmedia project is one that uses the strengths of each medium and matches them to the right kind of substory. Not every story is best told via film, or via comics, or via games. Transmedia allows us, as writers, to say that the detail around the backstory is way too heavy for the film, but just right for an interactive book so let's explore it there.

Bearing in mind that the examples above are all big

existing franchises (the *Star Wars* universe also explores some stories via transmedia) what are the opportunities for jobbing writers looking to survive? There are three ways that transmedia can work for you.

First, transmedia projects are rarely written by a single writer. The project is just too big. This therefore offers an excellent chance for a writer for hire to pick up some work. This is usually for one of two reasons: the main writer has either no time, or no writing experience in some of the media.

For example, the main writer could be a novelist who has never written a webisode. If you've written short-form film content in the same genre, maybe you can help. Or sometimes more writers are needed to speed things up.

> *For the first season of Psychoville we wrote a lot of background character detail for the accompanying website, which we won a BAFTA for. For the second season, we just couldn't find the time and had to get help.*

Reece Shearsmith and Steve Pemberton
Psychoville

A lot of transmedia projects need everything to go live at once: websites, webisodes on YouTube, podcasts, films – that's a lot of writing. Often it can't be scheduled out neatly, it all bunches up together. Again, this is where jobbing writers can seek out work.

So that's the first way that transmedia can offer opportunities to writers, by creating additional content for larger, existing transmedia projects. But there's a second way, and that's using transmedia in your own independent projects. Some media are relatively cheap to create content for: websites, podcasts, prose, webisodes.

An example of this is from my own project, Mr Vista. This was primarily a web series that ran for three series. However, I discovered that it was the spin-off material that people remembered. I did downloads, a little spoof game, printouts, emoticon sets – lots of things. Anything really that would take the downbeat geeky work-based Mr Vista ethos out into the real world.

The third way writers can use transmedia is to write elements to help make their own traditional projects more exciting to producers. A famous example is the horror film that texted the audience on the way home with the message "You didn't think it was over did you?" from the horror villain. If you replied you got a short bonus epilogue.

A few years back I consulted on a horror project that was being delivered via Twitter. It could have been a low-budget feature. But by delivering it via Twitter, which was still quite fresh, it gained much more publicity than "just another low-budget feature".

There are lots of other transmedia developments unfolding all the time, such as Alternate Reality Games (ARGs) and other ideas that link social media, live theatre and geotagging. A few places are now setting up to help content creators explore this field. Check out the annual conference Power to the Pixel which charts new media and innovations. If you want help automating your transmedia story (automatically send emails from your characters to people who sign up, etc.) then check out the work of Rob Pratten at UK-based Transmedia Storyteller.

http://www.tstoryteller.com

FACTUAL/REALITY SHOWS

This is a growing market for writers – but a hidden one. Why? Because the producers don't really want everyone to know that behind the scenes writers are creating storylines and material. One of the best adverts we saw in *Variety* was for a writer for the WWE Wrestling. Hey, *someone* has to write this stuff!

The advice here is the same as we've given elsewhere. Only try to enter the factual/reality market if you love the material already; you can't fake it. And think about what the producers would be looking for and what you can bring.

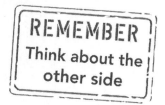

REMEMBER
Think about the other side

GAGS

Gag writing has a long tradition for writers. Woody Allen started out by writing jokes for Ed Sullivan. There's still a role for gag writers today as comedians need more material than ever, and it needs to be topical, too. Comedy writing of this nature is normally a deep specialism with writers focusing on delivering this kind of content across lots of media and formats; for example, writing a stand-up gag and a cartoon and some topical jokes for an after-dinner speech all in one day. It used to be a case of approaching people in need of regular funny lines and getting them to give you a go. The modern route seems to be setting up a Twitter account and just going for it! But on the plus side, radio and TV sketch shows consistently accept material from new writers. Radio comedy shows in particular often request for sketches to be submitted (to fit their brief), so stay across what's out there!

SPEECHWRITING

You may feel this is a dying art as more and more people write their own speeches now. But there are opportunities in speechwriting, should the area appeal. Speeches don't occur just in politics (where in fact they've given way to sound bites) but also in business and other major events where someone needs to give a key address.

Two bits of good news if you fancy exploring this avenue:

1 – One of the key factors of a good speech is a personal story told well. Solid storytelling techniques.

2 – Maybe the sound bite has replaced the long-form speech. But someone still needs to write those sound

bites. In this way, the job is very similar to the writing of gags!

Finding work in this area can be difficult, however, and would only be recommended for those who have an "in" with a certain business sector or audience.

Tim is often involved with the UK Speechwriters' Guild. Here are four speechwriting techniques that he's learned.

1 – Contrast, starting with a negative

Best example: "Ask not what your country can do for you, but what you can do for your country." Simple to emulate, too. As in: "You turn if you want to, the lady's not for turning."

2 – Puzzle, pause, solution

Start with something that doesn't make sense to get the audience's attention, then offer a captivating solution. What we, in script terms, would call a "set up and reveal". This is the kind of technique that can get that polite laughter from a conference crowd.

3 – Rule of three

Put things in threes to make a point: Life, liberty and the pursuit of happiness. The longest point normally goes last. An interesting experiment is to try and break this rule in conversation and see what happens. Say two things and people will wait for a third – until you have to say "and so on". Say four things and people will interrupt after three.

4 – Simple words for us

If you listen to the speeches of Winston Churchill he uses the simpler words (which happen to be the old English words) when talking about the British. These are words from childhood, easy words. Using these words takes us right back to early experiences – "fight", "beach", "dog".

When he talks about the enemy he uses more complex words. Words like "mechanised", "machinery", "invaders". These are harder words for the brain to process. The brain prefers the "hero words".

NICHE OPPORTUNITIES

Some career ideas you may not have fully explored:

1 – Web series
Fast-moving, short content, you can start today.

2 – Comics
Telling visual stories.

3 – Transmedia
A cutting-edge form of story, with no rules as yet but many ways forward.

4 – Factual/Reality
An "invisible" role, but one that's in demand.

5 – Gags
For those who plan to specialise in comedy.

6 – Speechwriting
Tricky to get into unless you have an "in".

REACHING OUT

> *Contacts get you in.*
>
> *But talent will keep you in.*

Doug Chamberlin
Writer
Toy Story 2

So far we've looked at a lot of opportunities for writers. But how do you take advantage of them? How do you reach out to people within the industry and let them know what you can do? That's what we look at in this chapter.

4 GOLDEN RULES

1 – Be normal

Take a step back and think: How do I communicate with someone else at a human level, just two professionals discussing a project? Not as a crazed, passionate, self-obsessed writer trying to impose themselves on someone they see as a walking pile of cash!

2 – Dialogue, not monologue

REMEMBER
Think about the other side

Your conversations with anyone in the industry should be just that, conversations. You should be listening as much as you are talking, showing an interest in their projects as well as expounding the benefits of yours.

3 – Talk slower

The ideas you're outlining are well known to you, so you talk through them fast. This could be coupled with the desire to just get the damn thing said quickly. This is akin to the man who decides to drive home at top speed because his brakes are broken. Slower means you look more confident *and* you are less likely to trip over your tongue and come across like a gabbling fool.

4 – Listen, really listen

Listen to what the other person says. And that means *really* listen. Not listen out for the things that you want to hear and ignore the rest of it. Listen to tone and watch body language, too.

One thing it took me a while to get used to was commenting on someone's body language or other feedback. For example, "You've glazed over as I've been talking about this project, is this not your kind of thing?" At first I was reticent to ask such a question, it seemed rude. But in fact the exact opposite is true, asking is of benefit to everyone. For me, it silences the concerned voice in my head: "Why aren't they listening, why have they glazed over, is this idea total rubbish?" If I try and continue talking, that voice gets louder and I start to make all sorts of assumptions about why they don't seem to like what I'm saying. Maybe the real reason is that they've remembered their car park ticket is about to run out! Asking is also of benefit to the person I'm talking to, it shows them I am paying attention and it also invites them to give me feedback. Maybe the project isn't their genre. Maybe they've heard three ideas like this today. Again, I only know by asking. Making assumptions and ploughing through often leads to misunderstandings, confusion and worry.

PITCHING

You need to practise it. There's a big difference between thinking you know it and having it on a scrap of paper – and saying it out loud. But let's take a tip from our actor friends. When they learn lines, they rehearse. They don't just read the script and then start performing. How could they? That would be stupid! Wouldn't it? Some people are just lucky at pitching. But isn't it true: the more you practise, the luckier you get.

People use all sorts of methods and techniques to put together their pitch. But how often do we think about what the pitch is supposed to do? What is its job? Only if we understand what it's supposed to do can we decide if ours will do it – or not!

The pitch has to be "pass-on-able"

The person you tell your story to has to tell other people the same pitch. Simple as that. It must be retainable and repeatable. Simple, but hard to test. Unless you use this pitch exercise:

1. You get together with a scriptwriting chum.

2. You tell them your pitch.

3. They tell you theirs.

4. You check that each one takes no more than two minutes.

5. Then you repeat the other person's pitch back to them, and they repeat yours back to you.

6. You see if they are repeated accurately. Were the important elements in there? Were incorrect elements added?

7. Rework as necessary. But you can't try it again with the same person for obvious reasons.

The clever part of this exercise is that you actually check if the pitch works. It doesn't matter how clever or clear you think it is. If the other person can't remember it and repeat it, it doesn't work. Redo it.

> *For TV, include in your pitch what kind of channel is it for, what time, what audience. It needs to fit into a recognisable place in the schedule.*

Chris Hill
Contributing Writer
Skins

Pitch checklist

When pitching, use this checklist to see if you are fully prepared.

- Research the company you are going to pitch to.
- Research the person you are going to meet.
- Introduce yourself first, then your project's title, logline, and then a brief summary of the story.
- Leave a one-pager, if requested.

WHAT'S A LOGLINE?

A logline is a one-sentence summary of what your story is about (certainly no more than two sentences!).

A good logline can really entice someone into the story (like a good 25 words or fewer pitch) and will usually indicate some basic plotting and structure that you would expect to see in the script. With this in mind, it's a really good idea for a writer to think of their logline before they start writing their screenplay. It helps crystallise the concept and story so that the writer can remain focused on what needs to be told throughout the writing process.

One template for a good logline goes something like

this: "It's about (a character/characterisation) who (action/desire/goal) but (conflict/the thing that's getting in their way)."

Some examples

"The civilian son of a mafia boss tries to protect his family after his father is critically wounded in a mob hit but finds himself dragged into the family business's corruption and power."

"A young farmhand on a distant planet joins the battle against the universe's evil forces but doesn't realise that his family's dark secret will have serious repercussions for him and his friends."

"A highly strung mother won't allow her children to leave the house but when three disconcerting housekeepers turn up to help her, strange events occur that suggest the house is haunted."

"A mild-mannered Englishman begins to wonder if he'll ever meet the woman of his dreams when he always attends weddings as a guest, never the groom, but when he meets a sexy American woman, he decides to pursue her as she could be the one to lead him up the aisle."

If you were pursuing these ideas as original screenplays,

the loglines would help you develop what absolutely needs to happen in the story. In other words, it would help shape the structure or give you more ideas on how to expand the plot. Looking at *The Godfather* logline above (you knew that, right?), in the script you would know that an attempted assassination would have to take place, and that this would be quite exciting and dramatic, and be a pivotal moment in the whole story.

A good logline is crucial. It's how your story can be summed up in a neat one or two sentences (sounds prescriptive and annoying but that's the way it is), which will then be used by everyone who has to pitch your script to their bosses, and their bosses' bosses, etc.

A logline is not to be confused with a "tagline" which is the marketing strap below your title on the poster to indicate some intrigue or hook about the film. "In space no one can hear you scream" was *Alien*'s famous tagline, but its logline would be something like: "A modest space cargo crew respond to a distress signal but are forced to confront a deadly alien which infiltrates their ship, leaving only one of the female members of the crew to fend for herself."

Loglines don't necessarily have to follow the well-worn template of "it's about a character who blah blah", but generally it helps to express a story in its simplest and most effective form as this is what audiences are really after. They don't want to be confused, they don't want to be misled, they don't want to be dazzled by your theme of Spanish paella through the 1800s, they just want to know what's going on, who's doing it and why.

PITCH YOURSELF!

How to answer the question: "What do you do?" or "Tell me about yourself."

Why do these questions get asked in the first place? Well, people want to work with people they like and know. They have to like *you* as well as your work. You'd be the same. You'd want to work with people you got on with, too.

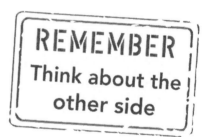

REMEMBER
Think about the other side

But "tell me about yourself, what do you do?" can be a hard question to answer sometimes. You could say, "I'm a writer." Is that the whole story though? Does that mean that people won't find out about your directing? What if you're in a room full of writers and want to stand out?

The right answer!

Here are three pieces of advice that may set you on your way to having an effective answer at your fingertips. Use these three ideas to help you start brainstorming. Then afterwards we'll look at how to structure these raw thoughts.

1 – What, how, why

Don't just think about *what* you do (writing for the screen) but also think about *how* you do it (certain genres, certain techniques you specialise in such as dialogue or visual writing) and then also consider *why*. Why did you become a writer? The "why" can often be the part people remember, as it's most personal.

2 – Ask others

Ask other people how they would describe you. They may use words you wouldn't. And they may value things you do that you don't value. It can be very insightful.

3 – Realise this won't work 100% of the time

Whatever you come up with, it won't be a magic bullet phrase that always works and sums up your life in 10 words. What you are actually seeking is a clear way to get your foot in the door. Then you can talk about the full range of your talents. If it's about 80% on the nose, that's going to be useful.

Structure

How might you structure a pitch about yourself? Use three sentences.

First sentence: Write about your key achievements or successes, or what you have going for you.

"I am a BAFTA-nominated writer and winner of the Jerwood Film Prize whose last film was screened at the Edinburgh Film Festival."

OR

"I am a recent graduate from the London Film School and my final short was in the top 10 on Virgin Media Shorts last year."

Second sentence: Write about yourself and your interests.

"Recently I've become very interested in new technologies and new ways of telling stories."

OR

"Even though I've graduated I remain a student of new narrative structures and techniques."

Third sentence: Write about the future and your goals.

"My next project combines my writing experience with new technology as it is an interactive novel for iOS and Android that is using a brand new story engine."

OR

"Now I'm keen to get out into the real world of work and bring my energy and effort to some interesting projects."

Remember – this is just the paragraph about yourself. You still need to match this to what you know are *their* goals and *their* projects.

A GOOD INTRODUCTORY EMAIL

Today, most approaches to people are via email. We send emails every day and it's become second nature. Here are six tips on writing a good email.

1 – Keep it short

When it was a letter, then one, nicely spaced and not cramped side of A4 was the norm. And yes, shrinking your font size to 10 points and expanding your margins to fit more on a page *was* cheating. Nowadays, we would suggest an email letter is half this length or even less. Whoever is reading it doesn't have much time. Demonstrate to them that you know how to catch people's attention with few words – after all, that's what you're selling! Do them a favour (by not wasting their time) and they might do you a favour (by wanting to find out more about you and your script).

2 – Boast

We're a modest bunch, us writers. Everything is "quite good" and "nearly there". Now is not the time for this kind of talk. If you've won something, then get it in there NOW! If your script is great, then say it is. As long as you can back it up with facts. Boasting is not the same as arrogance. Be proud of what you've achieved.

3 – What do you want?

"Why am I reading this? What do you want?" It's surprising how few people bear this in mind when sending their introductory email. What, specifically, are you asking the person you're approaching to do? Does your request sound reasonable? Does it sound like you have sought them out or is it a cut-and-paste job? Tailor your email to the reader, make it clear what you want, make your request easy to grant. For example: "I read about your new film in *Screen International*. I am also writing a sci-fi love story. It would be great to meet up at (location near to you) for half an hour to hear about your experiences, particularly with regards to how you managed to make the dialogue jargon-free, a challenge I am struggling with."

Bonus tip: If you re-read your email from the other person's point of view and it seems unsure or generic, then you need to make what you want clearer.

4 – Be positive

In the example above it says "it would be great to meet up" rather than "would you like to meet?" A small point, but one that shows you are 100% up for the meeting rather than wanting to do it if they don't mind doing it.

5 – What's in it for them?

Why should they bother to meet you or email you back or give you work? What's so great about you? Find it. And write it in. Check out tip (2) again!

6 – Write well

For God's sake, you're a writer, not a lotto spam merchant. Don't misspell words or use poor grammar, or worse, get the person's name wrong in the letter itself. Be brief and to the point. Three paragraphs should do: intro, the purpose of contacting the producer/company, and round-up/farewell.

Honestly, there's so much you can tell about a writer from the way they style an email/letter, so take time to word it carefully, and be happy with its tone and delivery.

USING THE PHONE/SKYPE

You may be tempted to skip over this section. "Who uses the phone these days?"

That's the very reason you *should* use the phone. It retains the benefits it always had:

- It's immediate.
- It's more conversational.
- It causes fewer misunderstandings than email.
- It's two-way.
- It's cheaper than meeting in person.

But now it has the added benefit of not many people using it. We're all so busy emailing each other and ignoring emails from other people that the phone has been forgotten.

Perhaps the only downside to the phone lies in its immediacy. You can email someone, then follow it up with more information later, then try a different approach with your third attempt. Not so with the dog and bone; if you get through to the caller, then you have to hit the ground running. If you want to make those calls count, here are a few simple tips.

- Make the call at a good time; not when it's noisy, not just before someone will visit you, not when you're in a place with a dodgy signal or bad Wi-Fi for Skype.

- Jot down some notes of what you want to say; not a script, just some bullet points. Ironically, it can be when a call is going well that we forget to say some of our key points. Also prepare what to say if you need to leave a message, either on the answer machine or with someone else.

- Introduce yourself. Say your name and who you are *clearly*. With an email, they can ponder who you are for a while and it doesn't matter. On the phone, you don't want to be 30 seconds into your conversation and they're still mulling over exactly who you are. You could say something like: "Hi, Mr Producer. It's Mr Writer here. You liked my short film at the Hamburg Film Festival, the one with the time-travelling dog."

- Warm your voice up first. Sometimes, if you've not spoken in a while as you've been typing away for a few hours, your voice can almost dry up. Just say a few words before you pick up the phone.

- Continue to follow the golden rules: speak slowly, really listen, keep a dialogue going, and be normal!

- Stand up (physically) for the call. It seems an odd thing to do, but it makes you speak more clearly and you will sound more professional.

Skype

All of the above points apply to Skype too, except for the last one. Instead of standing up, sit up straight. This helps with your voice in the same way, but also makes you look attentive. It goes without saying (just about) that the room behind you should be tidy.

Occasionally you can get audio feedback with Skype. Have a pair of headphones handy in case you need to use them. Hunting for them mid-conversation ruins your flow.

SOCIAL NETWORKING

A lot of writers/producers/editors/execs are on Facebook or Twitter. Interact with them, and start building an online correspondence. One tweet to someone saying, "please read my script!" will (rightly) go ignored. But regular tweets that interact with the person's timeline may generate a more personal response, and yield positive results somewhere down the line.

Have you written/made a short film yet? No? Hmm. If a producer Googled you, would any result show a link to writing or previous creative achievements? No? Hmm. A radio script? A stage play? Something you did at college or for a friend? *Something* that makes you stand out in your chosen field rather than just a ranty timeline on Twitter? We're not only talking about your online presence, it's all the other things you could or should be doing in real life that will inevitably spill online, and get you noticed or help your profile.

NETWORKING EVENTS

Network. Network wherever you can. Festivals, screenings, courses, talks. Attend. Chat to other writers. Say hello to the guest speaker. Be nice. Be proactive.

Always be doing something. Don't get stuck in a rut. It's good to get out of the house every once in a while. Blogging has become a useful way to network with fellow writers and like-minded individuals. They may be people who won't advance your career (although y'never know!) but it's nice to make some friends and not feel so isolated.

Use your common sense. Think laterally. Someone from Working Title may be doing a Q&A or attending a pitching event, so mark it down on your calendar, go along and network. Try to introduce yourself to the main person, but be just as nice to and interested in everyone else, including the coatroom guy. Someone from your favourite production company could be at a BAFTA talk. Go up and say hello. Ask them if they'll agree to read your stuff (which becomes a solicited script!). Even if they won't, they might remember your name when your unsolicited script comes across their desk.

And here's the bonus part of going to such events: even if you don't meet the main person, you've still got a way above average chance of meeting someone you'll get on with. Why? Because they've attended the event for the same reason you have, to see someone they admire give a talk. You have a shared interest.

Remember the golden rules we started this chapter with. Be normal, have a nicely paced dialogue and really listen to what other people are saying.

I have a theory about networking. And that's that meeting someone and giving them a card and following up later will never lead to anything. What? Then why bother? Because I think work only really starts to flow once you've met someone three or four times. Of course, you need that first meeting to go well in order for people to remember you in a positive manner for the next time. But don't expect one meeting or one conversation to lead directly to anything in the short term.

Business cards

When you go to a networking event, everyone's advice is to hand out your cards and network. Then the "fog of conferences" descends.

You have dozens of cards. Who was who? What did you talk about? Who the hell is Jane and why do you have her card?

A memorable card, linked to you in some way, is a good idea. A card can be a way of showing that you can bring creativity to an established format, or that you can intrigue people while at the same time delivering the pertinent information.

But don't go too crazy and don't go too cheap.

Formal networking events

Some networking events have a structure to them and are more formal in nature. This can often discourage new writers from attending. In fact, the opposite should be true. A networking event with a formal structure can help take the worry out of what you should be doing, and enables you to focus on your objectives.

A typical structure is:

- Arrival and mingle time (always arrive early before people form their own little huddles that are hard to penetrate)

- Quick introductions from everyone in the room (prepare what you're going to say or risk wasting that chance to pitch to everyone at once)

* Sit-down meal, snacks or drinks (sit in the middle of a table where you can chat to five people)

* Guest speaker session (ask a question in the Q&A part if you can, but don't use this as an opportunity to hog the limelight)

* Informal ending (remember to catch up with people you want to speak to, this is where handing out your business card really counts)

WRITERS' FESTIVALS

Quite a few networking events are free to attend, while others are inexpensive Q&As or screenings. Festivals can be more costly in comparison, but provide great opportunities to pitch, mingle and generate new contacts. This is because they are longer – typically one to three days – and more in-depth.

"New contacts" are to be cultivated wisely. Don't just email them after the event – "nice to meet you!" – and file their business card away. If the situation allows, try to maintain contact every few months or so, find out what they're doing or update them on your projects. Alternatively, if you meet the new contact at a future networking event, it will result in them having more awareness of and familiarity with you, which can lead to work!

Here are some of the major events we like to check out on a regular basis:

- The London Screenwriters' Festival is *the* major networking event of the year for screenwriters everywhere, new or experienced.

Check out the great speakers at LSF
http://www.londonscreenwritersfestival.com/

- BAFTA talks/events host a variety of screenings, Q&As and networking opportunities (subscribe to their newsletter to keep up to date).

See what BAFTA has to offer
http://www.bafta.org/film/events

The BFI London Film Festival has really come on in recent years, with many more events and Q&As in addition to the screenings of new films. Check out the BFI website regularly as they have different events spread throughout the year.

BFI has a special London Film Festival page
http://www.bfi.org.uk/lff

SHORT FILM FESTIVALS

There are hundreds of short film festivals up and down the country (and internationally) but keep an eye out for Raindance, Bristol Brief Encounters, London Short Film Festival, Leeds International Film Festival, and London Independent Film Festival.

A list of festivals
http://film.britishcouncil.org/festivals-directory

CANNES AND OTHER BUSINESS FESTIVALS

We've talked so far about events that focus on the writer and filmmaker. However, there are many industry festivals, all around the world, that instead focus on the business. Here we'll use the Cannes Film Festival and Film Market as an example (but this could equally be a television market like MIPCOM or a games event like Gamescom).

Cannes: what happens there?

Cannes is a great example of the inner conflict within the entertainment business. Film is both an art form and big business. What we call "Cannes" is in fact two events that sit side by side.

There's the film festival, where people watch the best films from around the world and the stars walk up the red carpet and it's all very glamorous.

But underneath the big cinemas is a trade show, the market, or *Marché du Film*. This is where the business happens.

All the films upstairs being shown at the festival are done deals. They have distribution already, the rights have pretty much all been snapped up. Downstairs is where the production companies and sales agents are trying to do other deals. Deals for mid-budget films, lower budget films and straight-to-DVD or straight-to-VOD. Horror films, kids' films, dramas, indie films – you name it. They have screenings all around town, to show their films to other business people and potential buyers. These films aren't in the festival or any competition; this is purely a marketing exercise to license the finished films around the world. A lot of the large hotels, like the Carlton and the Grand, almost become part of the market, with companies using their rooms as offices.

To support both the festival and the market there is a series of pavilions, with most countries represented. The UK Pavilion is a good place to meet people, sit down, pick up news and flyers, etc.

Why go as a writer?

Firstly, it's worth seeing the business operate in this way. To see films being bought in terms of "Have you got 10 different horror films I can sell in the German DVD market?" is eye-opening. We can be precious about our scripts, but this is the reality of the process if we want to get our films out there.

Secondly, everyone is there. OK, they may be there to do these kinds of deals and not to chat to us, but they are there all the same. It often seems easier to get a meeting with a UK company while they're in Cannes than to meet up in London where the meeting gets endlessly put back and shifted. While people are in

Cannes, they're in the "meetings vibe" and plan to do little else. Take a slice of that action. Not many writers go, so you stand out.

How do I get in?

This is important, don't just rock up for the week and hope to wing it. You probably won't get in. Festival registration and obtaining a badge are a prerequisite to attend. As a writer, there are three badges to choose from.

1 – A festival badge. This gets you into the film festival events only, not the market. But that's not so bad as you can still use the pavilions and get into most areas. However, it can be slightly limiting for those writers who really want to meet a lot of people as you can't get into all the business venues.

2 – A market badge. This is almost an "all areas" badge. You can attend the festival and also go into all the hotels, the market and see market screenings. On the downside, it's expensive and can be tricky to obtain. It costs about €300 for the full duration (prices alter so check carefully); cheaper three-day and one-day badges are also available. Some people find the badges difficult to get as you must prove you're in the film industry. That's understandable: this is a

professional market for business people. If you have an agent, then a letter from them is fine; an IMDb credit usually counts, too. If you feel you don't qualify for the market badge, take this as a sign that you would probably be wasting your money attending at this stage of your career; aim to attend when you have more work under your belt.

3 – Short Film Corner badge. Cannes also supports short films via a small "Corner" of the market. If you enter a short, you can get badges for two people for about €80! These get you into the market areas but not the screenings. For a lot of people this is the right badge: it offers the sweet spot of affordability and gets TWO people into the festival. Of course you need a short film to enter, but it doesn't have to be an awesome film. They don't judge these for quality or appraise them. It just needs to look half decent.

How to get the most out of it

If you have the full market badge or the Short Film Corner badge, you get access to a large online database of festival delegates that you can browse beforehand. This is a vital tool. You can search by country and by activity; for example, you can search for all the production companies coming from Australia. You can then drill down into past productions and discover what they're trying to sell at this market.

To arrange a meeting, simply email the person or production company you'd like to approach. Don't delay – waiting until you get to Cannes is too late, people's diaries are full by then.

If you aim for the right level of contact, you can set up a lot of meetings. I find I get about 20–25% of the meetings I want. My only tip around this is that a lot of people ignore the first email, assuming it's a bulk email or from someone taking a random chance. About half of the meetings I get are arranged because I send a second email to follow up. That's why I usually start arranging my Cannes diary about six weeks beforehand.

Book your accommodation and flights as early as possible as prices increase. For those doing it super cheap, there's a campsite, or you can look at hotels that are out of town. Going as a group can often be cheaper as you can get a four-bed apartment, for example.

What should you take?

In short, not very much. No one wants to take anything from you, as they'll have to take it back home on a plane. Business cards are good. Maybe some one-pagers, which you keep in a folder to use as pitching aids.

If you have a film, bring a couple of DVDs – but hand out a Vimeo link instead, perhaps on a glossy flyer. Less is more. What's essential is keeping good notes yourself. Who are you meeting, when, what about and what did you agree?

What happens after?

Cannes is a great opportunity to lift your visibility and increase your gravity. As a writer, you won't be doing deals. But you will meet people who need your services, as a rewriter or a reader. It's unlikely you'll get interest in your spec scripts, but it's possible. More likely is that people will want to use your skills to move their own projects forward.

Remember: Cannes is a high-profile example but the above advice goes for all festivals and industry events.

OTHER EVENTS

You know what stops all these writers' events from being great? All the other writers. They keep hogging the speakers/execs and pitching their scripts! Joking aside, sometimes it can be a good idea to go to events where you'll be the "only writer in the village".

I go to the local MPs Business Breakfast meetings. I don't go primarily to pick up work directly, that would be too much of a long shot. But I go to make sure the local great and good know who I am and what I do. Over the years this has given me "first dibs" on some local, but quite profitable, pieces of work.

Maybe try to network at actors' events, or go to producers' meetings, or visit seminars on speechwriting. The overlap is greater than you think, especially if you write more than just screenplays and branch out into other areas – as we advocate in this book. If you're more of a writer/director, then go to local creative hook-ups and business events, or social gatherings where marketing companies meet – maybe they need a director for their adverts.

STAYING IN TOUCH

All of this networking activity counts for nothing unless you do something with the contacts you collect. Here are some handy pointers.

1 – Put your new contacts in an address book of some sort. It doesn't matter if this is on the cloud, your phone or your PC. But back it up or make sure it backs itself up. Your contacts are your currency and are valuable.

2 – Send a "hello" email, text, tweet or phone call to say, well, "hello". Maybe a recap of what you talked about, where you met and any links to what you discussed. This keeps it personal and memorable. Brevity is the key word here. For bonus points, include a question. A question is harder to ignore, as it needs an answer. Without one, the recipient can read but then ignore the email.

3 – Follow up. Not straight away, not the next day. Leave it a while, usually a month or so. When you follow up, mention what has happened in the intervening time, either related to the project or to your career. That way, you're showing that things are moving and dynamic, creating a sense of urgency. Top tip – put a

reminder in your calendar/email programme of when to follow up.

4 – Three times and then out. There seems little point in sending more than three messages to someone who doesn't reply. Move on. Don't hold a grudge though. They're probably busy with other projects and may come back to you eventually when they have something they feel you could help with.

5 – Create an email list to help you keep in touch long term with people you may work with only very occasionally. Use this list once a year or so, when you have key news to impart or a big event coming up. Think carefully about who you add to this list as you don't want to spam people and create a negative impression.

6 – Everyone's a contact. Not everyone you meet and get on with will be in a position to help you. What do you do – walk away with a carefree shrug? No. Be normal. They're an interesting person, so keep in touch anyway. Maybe they know someone who can help you move your projects along. And maybe you know someone who can help move theirs.

7 – Remember to keep all your contact activity two-way. "Dialogue, not monologue." It's better to give than to receive. Offer help as well as ask for it.

> *There is a phrase, start at the bottom and work up. People often try to get in touch with people low down in an organisation and then network their way from there. With our film we did the opposite, we went to the people at the top. They don't do the work of course or even make the specific decisions. However, if you work in middle management and you get a message from your boss to check out a film you are more likely to do it than if the same message comes up from someone lower than you.*

Chris Musselwhite
Independent Producer

YOU DON'T NEED TO MEET NEW PEOPLE AT ALL

Sometimes you know enough people. They just don't know enough about you. Approaching new people can be daunting. Talking to people you already know, less so. Use your existing contacts. Do they know *fully* about *all* your skills? One way to make sure they do is use a "window of opportunity". It's a bit of a corporate name for what is basically a spreadsheet, and it's dead simple. Across the top – all your clients / customers / contacts etc. Down the side – all your services: script reading, directing, rewrites, guest blogging, whatever it is that you do.

This makes a grid. Put a tick where you've done work already. If you've done script reading for company X, put a tick in that box. And so on.

For most people, this reveals a disappointing result. Most of the window is empty – no ticks. But it also presents a lot of opportunity that's easy to act upon and you can start straight away.

Get in touch. It's not difficult. It's not cold calling. It's just speaking to people, *people you already know*, and saying: "Do you know I do this as well? Can I tell you more?" Try it!

START YOUR OWN EVENT

What if there isn't an event near you, or not quite the one you want? Then start one. Upon first consideration, this seems like a lot of work. It needn't be, however, if you focus on something small and well targeted, and use helpful free online tools. The benefit of starting your own event is that it puts you at the heart of the networking opportunity. If you find it tricky to mingle at other events, then a situation where everyone already knows about you when they turn up can be very appealing. Guests come up to you rather than you having to approach them. A few examples:

- Tim used to help organise a local short film festival. Publicised almost exclusively by word of mouth and with no funding, it still drew in 200 people to see no-budget shorts.

- Our friend Suki Singh arranged a series of screenings for his low-budget feature, *Emulsion*, and either introduced the film or gave a Q&A.

- Danny did a very small-scale but focused series of events, meeting up with followers of his blog and other bloggers. This put a face to the name and allowed conversations that had started online to go much deeper.

- Tim holds a series of local networking events for writers and filmmakers, just people he knows, with every invited guest allowed to bring a colleague or two who would also benefit. Very simple, but they've led to some long-term collaborations.

When you think about "an event", you may envisage something large that costs money – both to set up and to attend. But it doesn't have to be like that.

Get a free venue (a room above a pub, etc.) and use Meetup or Facebook Events to track your attendees. Charging is usually not worth it: it puts some people off and you'll probably regret the effort required to scrape in a few quid. A better way is "go free", get as many folks as possible there and send a hat round if you need to cover anything. It's generally more advantageous to have 100 people who are really happy to chip in a few quid each than 10 people who have paid £5 and are wondering why they did.

REACHING OUT

Some top tips from this chapter

1 – Practise your pitch

Team up with another writer if that helps.

2 – Pitch yourself

Your work extends beyond a single script, so think about how you would pitch yourself.

3 – Virtual communications

We can all sharpen up on our online correspondence, including Skype calls and emails.

4 – Be in the room at events

Don't just attend networking events and festivals – get the most out of them. Or start your own.

5 – Follow up

Follow up with the contacts you make!

Money and Business

BALANCING "NORMAL WORK" AND WRITING

" I'd get home from working all day, sitting at a desk, to sit at another desk and write. And I did that for months and months. That's why I don't have any patience for people who say they have a full-time job and don't have any time to write. If you've got time to watch TV, to read, you have time. "

James Moran

Even if we take on board James's advice and give up certain things in order to devote time to writing, it can be tough to balance your "normal work" and your writing time.

Our only advice around this is that routine helps. That could be a set day or a set time of the day. If your work life is more irregular, then allocating so many minutes a day or so many hours a week could suit you. The key thing is to track it or diarise it.

The other tip is to try to find "invisible time".

When we were shooting Who Killed Nelson Nutmeg? *I still had some other writing to do. So I got up two hours early every day just to ensure it was done, and then had the rest of the day free to focus on the film.*

GOING FREELANCE

Life is more complicated than just saying, "I'm giving up my job and going to be a writer." There are numerous considerations and practicalities involved, all unique and with varying significance to each person who's about to go freelance. "Is my other half going to hit the roof? How will I buy food and clothes for my two-year-old son? Who will pay for Dad's medical treatment? What is the least I can earn that will ensure I can pay my way? How can I guarantee some sort of income? Will I ever socialise again? What will my friends think? How am I going to afford the wedding? Will I miss a payment on the car? On the loan? Should I sell my flat/house? Maybe I should move back in with Mum. Should I move to Hollywood? Am I nuts?"

There are no easy answers, but, despite it all, the dream of writing for film and/or TV will usually win through, and will guarantee its own set of problems and frustrations as the effort inevitably takes its toll on your life and relationships. However, fate will sometimes offer you a glimmer of hope or keep a foot in the door of destiny so that all your effort and sacrifice (and that of your loved ones) doesn't go to waste. It takes time, it takes effort, it takes talent and it takes luck; a crapshoot of determination and chance that will either make or break you but will nearly always be worth the effort, no matter what the outcome.

And hey, at least you gave it a go!

Making the decision to go freelance, in any profession, is a risky and exciting prospect. But it's essential to have a good idea of what's ahead of you or what you're up against if you're going to realise your dream.

When is the right time?

Many of us have naturally good storytelling instincts, but they don't necessarily translate into successful writing or a successful writing career. How do you realistically assess the possibilities? The answers to the following questions will either reassure you about what lies ahead or make you doubt whether it's quite the right time.

* Has a reputable producer optioned one of my scripts?
* Have I won or placed in any script awards?
* Have I got an agent?
* Have I written or directed a short film?
* A radio play?
* Or theatre?
* Have I received any feedback that suggests other people value my work and indicates that I'm on the right track?
* Am I reading other people's scripts and learning more about technique?
* Can I genuinely see an improvement in my style of craft and story?
* Do I tell stories with commercial potential or are

they more personal stories with limited appeal?

* Do I know the market/industry well enough to understand how my scripts will be received?
* Do I make broad assumptions about the industry and then complain about the system when really I have no first-hand knowledge of what's going on?
* Am I getting tired of it all?
* Am I making enough money?
* Is it worth it?
* Can I do it?

It's a lot to consider, and even the questions that generate a negative response won't necessarily mean it's time to jack it all in. However, they will be a good indicator of how you're progressing and what needs to be done to make writing a more viable choice of career for you. There are absolutely no guarantees. Talk is not only cheap, it's free. You can only go so far on encouragement and half-promised deals.

Think about this before you go freelance

As this book has already explained, being a working writer is about more than just doing the writing. Imagine you have some really good film or one-off scripts written and some spec TV scripts and other treatments all completed. (You can write these before you go freelance, after all.) Now imagine it's day one of your freelance life. What are you going to do that day? Write? No, you have the material you need already. Your efforts will probably be focused on finding work. Who are you going to phone up? What meetings can you start to arrange? If you don't know, you aren't ready, you aren't connected enough.

FEES

To help you think about your possible life as a professional freelance writer, this section looks at the money involved.

UK film pay

If you find yourself in the lucky position of getting your feature script made, then you can expect to receive 1–2% of the film's budget. For example, if your film is going to cost £750k to make, you might receive £18,900 as your screenplay fee (an option/development fee will be separate, and development fees differ wildly, ranging from working for free to getting a few grand for your effort).

Be mindful of terms like "floor & ceiling payments". A

floor payment is the minimum fee you'll receive (which will be agreed with you, the producer and your agent). A ceiling payment is to cover the possibility of the budget increasing but you don't receive 1% of this higher budget. Instead, you receive an agreed maximum fee.

Television

These figures are from the good folk at the Writers' Guild of Great Britain (WGGB) so they represent the basic minimum rates for a new screenwriter (if you have experience/previous credits, your agent will no doubt negotiate a better fee). Work for smaller productions may not be part of the WGGB agreement so could be less. But it's always a useful point of reference from which to start payment discussions.

As a new writer, for BBC TV half-hour scripts (e.g. *Doctors*) you could expect to receive approximately £4,700. BBC TV hour scripts start at £10,800 while ITV hour scripts start at £12,650 (pro rata).

Fees for children's TV half-hour scripts will be similar to a BBC half-hour fee (as a minimum) but could be a couple of thousand pounds higher as they are often a "one-off fee" to include royalties and residuals (a royalty is a percentage of the sale price, a residual is a percentage of the original writing fee). It's common for kids' animated series to have 11-minute or 7-minute episodes. For these, you could expect to receive around £2,000 and £1,200 respectively.

For primetime TV drama, you can look forward to receiving a "first day of filming fee", which means you get your writing fee *again* when they start filming your script. But please note: this is only on TV hour-long dramas and some children's live-action shows, *not* animation or soap operas (where one-off/restricted payments are in place).

Get the full rundown of WGGB's basic rates
http://www.writersguild.org.uk/rates-agreements

INCOME STREAMS

Most writers will make money from a variety of sources. This variety is invaluable and gives you stability as circumstances change; it means all your eggs aren't in one basket. We've already talked about how to increase the breadth of your work via the "window of opportunity" idea.

However, keep tabs on the reality behind this spread of work. Which work is profitable? Which clients give you the best work? It's surprisingly easy to get it wrong. It's even easier to take your regular clients and your most profitable work for granted.

It's an often-quoted statement in the freelance world that people spend 80% of their effort chasing the 20% of their work that comes via new business. What if you put that effort into your regular gigs and impressing your existing clients? Or could you generate income through other freelance work, like proofreading or copy-editing, or writing articles, and so on?

Top tip – if you use a spreadsheet to keep track of your invoices, then try subdividing the list by client or activity. As the months progress, you'll see what is the most profitable work. It's then up to you to decide if you want to do more of that work, and reduce your hours, *or* diversify more.

WRITING FOR FREE

Much as it angers and frustrates writers, agents and the Writers' Guild, there simply is no getting around the fact that, at some stage, you're going to have to work for free. Even if you're a seasoned scribe, sometimes you just have to pucker up and do some pro bono work to help get a project off the ground.

It's not ideal, it's not fair, it's not perfect… but it's a fact. It's the reality of the business. And you know what, sometimes it's OK. Sometimes it's just simply necessary. Even in television, sometimes you'll be asked to do a free outline before they agree to commission you. This is usually two/three pages, but it can be a treatment of between six and ten pages. A treatment is a lot of work, especially for free, but if you want the commissioned gig, you're not going to walk away, right?

Most agents know that this is the norm, and occasionally projects get off the ground on the notion of good faith between the writer and producer. This is not for one second endorsing the idea that an eager writer agrees to a wily producer's demands, but there is a way to agree to do unpaid work without feeling manipulated, used or taken for granted.

First ask yourself: **do I like this project?** This is the most important. Forget money. Forget fame. Forget your Oscar speech. Do you dig the story? Does it grab your attention and get you excited? Or, can you make it work and enjoy yourself in the process even though it's not something that overtly thrills or moves you? If the subject matter can generate sufficient passion and interest, then it might be worthwhile taking on the work because it's something you believe in, and something that you think could eventually pay off.

Next, **do I like this producer?** Can you work with them? Do you know their credits? What's their experience? If they're new and ambitious, do you believe in their zeal and conviction? Does the plan for funding and development sound reasonable and promising? Agreeing to do unpaid work for a producer is enticing when you're an unknown screenwriter (hey, gotta get the CV going, right?) but if you're just doing it for the sake of it, then it's probably not going to work out.

Now, **what's the deal?** "I'm doing this work for free now, so what do I get later when it gets funding?" Can they agree a basic contract before you proceed because otherwise the producer gets what they want, you work hard, but if it falls through, then you get nothing. This is the tricky part. Producers won't want to involve your agent or get into contract talks until they get funding in place. Until then, you're acting on good faith and a verbal agreement, which may or may not be binding, depending on who witnessed the conversation. Still, some producers will agree to a basic one-letter contract that can protect your rights (and theirs), and keep everything above board. This gives peace of mind, but can be difficult to obtain.

If you're feeling uncertain, ask yourself: **do I trust this person?** If you don't know them at all, and have no prior relationship with them, then do you believe all the puffed up talk about agreements once funding is in place? If you don't feel right, then it's best not to get involved in the project.

When starting a new script, a lot of producers will tell you there's no money, that they can't pay you now but they'll pay you later. Yet, if they are a reputable producer with some credits or clout, then they should be able to pay you something, even if it's just a token few hundred pounds. Don't be afraid to ask.

It's a tough situation. They need you, the writer, but if you don't want to play ball, then they can easily find someone else to fill your shoes. They're in the powerful position of negotiation, to bend you into doing some unpaid writing. But while it's not the ideal situation for any writer, it is a common feature of everyday business. Don't say yes because you're desperate for any kind of break or exposure. Say yes when you feel happy that the project is interesting and could lead to something down the line, or if the producer is genuine and professional and it could be the start of a good relationship. Take it into consideration. Try to understand their situation. It's tough for them, too.

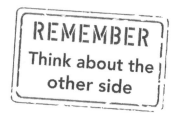

TAX

Obviously in this book we can't give tax advice.

But our golden rule is to keep some of your income put aside, preferably in a different bank account, for when you need to pay income tax on your earnings. This can be many months after you get paid (18 months later sometimes) so keeping a proportion safe, around 20%, ensures you won't get caught out.

Remember, you must inform HMRC as soon as you start working for yourself so they have you on their system. They will give you a special code (UTR number, which is different from your NI number) and will send you a tax form when it's due.

MAKE EFFORT VISIBLE

Don't be invisible.

Showing the effort behind your work enhances it, rather than diminishes it. Some people think that it's better to keep quiet about the working process, to suddenly reveal a finished masterpiece as if to say, "Look what I did with no effort."

I once took part in a corporate event with chef Gary Rhodes. Gary talked through his menu, highlighting the steps involved. He painted vivid pictures of every ingredient, articulating the various cooking methods. And, you know what, it made it taste better. Or at least made you think it tasted better. Which is the point. By talking about the process it made us all appreciate it more. I am aware this advice flies in the face of convention.

Be proud of your drafts. Be proud of your changes and rewrites. Be proud of your inspirations. And share them. It adds value to your work, or at the very least a sense of positive momentum!

MONEY AND BUSINESS – TOP TIPS

A recap of this chapter

1 – Have a plan to go freelance

Make sure this is a sensible plan based on your own circumstances. In the meantime, be rigorous in finding time for writing.

2 – Fees

Know what your work is worth against the market rate, in the field and medium you are working in.

3 – Know your sources of income

Keep an eye on where your money comes from. Are you spending most of your time chasing small pieces of work?

4 – Tax

Get registered. Put aside 20% of your earnings.

AGENTS

CRITICAL TO SUCCESS?

The most common complaint you'll hear from unrepresented writers is, "I can't get anyone to read my work. I need an agent. How do I get one?" While the most common remark from writers *with* agents is, "I generally source my own work."

Good writers get busy, and they develop a decent network of contacts, and this creates work. Agents help with all of this, of course, and they're a vital part of your professional profile. But if you don't have one yet, there's still plenty you can do to get noticed in the biz. Use your personality, talent and nous and start feeling the benefits, now.

DO YOU NEED ONE?

You don't need one. Well, you do (it's definitely preferable to have an agent), but until then, here's a secret: you can get by fine without one (Tim does!). Sure, it's a bit of a tougher graft, but you can organise meetings, introduce yourself to producers/companies and get your scripts out there, just like any agent would do on your behalf.

Get industry-savvy

Watch a lot of TV and films. Make a mental or written note of the key players: script editor, writer, producer, director, executive producers. Then send them your email/letter/query (not necessarily all of them, use your common sense).

You might catch them at the right time, or impress them with your approach, or they may be too busy. But if your request is any good, it should solicit some kind of response. If you haven't already, check out our section about sending a good email in the "Reaching Out" chapter.

Using your smarts

Once you're industry-savvy, you can start using your noggin to be extra clever about who you approach, and why. For example, maybe *Broadcast* has announced that CiTV have commissioned a new series from

Amazeballs Productions. What do you do? Email/write to the Amazeballs producer with your brilliant intro/query, and see what's going on.

Personal/industry smarts

A lot of people we meet in the biz have these three key traits in common: personality, talent, and a lot of industry nous/savvy. That's all *you* need to get by, too. In fact, a bit of personality and nous is all you need to get started; your personal talent will help you stay afloat. Then it might be time to get an agent!

HOW TO GET AN AGENT

The approach

* Do some work. It seems obvious, but have some great work under your belt. Can you do what you say you can? Then prove it!

* Write a letter outlining your work, your approach, your goals, how the agent can help you and how you will help them.

* Highlight artistic or commercial successes, e.g. awards or commissioned work, to make it easy for

them to say yes. Make it look like you're a person on the way up.

- Use contacts. A recommended contact counts for a lot. It puts you on the top of the pile. Can you get someone you know to recommend you to an agent? This will be your best chance.

- Name-drop. If you don't have a personal "in", then name-drop in your letter. Show you are part of the industry.

- One at a time. It's a small world that agents live in. Ideally, send out your prospective letter to one agent at a time. You shouldn't approach two or more agents from the same agency.

- Have your work ready. If your letter works, then have your spec material ready to go out in the best condition, best draft, best layout, etc.

- Be patient. Agents represent their clients. Looking for new clients is therefore low priority. Expect slow progress. This is an activity to do in the background. Writing and contacting other people in the biz are both more important anyway!

YOU'VE GOT AN AGENT, WHAT NEXT?

Once you do manage to nab an agent, get ready to sit

back and watch those assignments and offers roll in, right? Right?

If only it were so. Getting an agent is an important step in your career as it validates you as a writer. Then your name and work get known around town as the agent begins to do their spin. But while it's commonly accepted in America that an agent will get you work, here in the UK it's a wholly different matter. The reality is that having an agent is not a guarantee that you will get work, ever.

This is where the whole agent issue gets interesting. Before you had one, you couldn't get their interest because of your lack of work, but now you do have one, the situation hasn't changed much despite their best efforts to "get you out there".

Most successful scriptwriters will have found a way to work in the system regardless of representation or reputation. They will have wangled a TV deal of some sort, have written for a children's show, or done a radio play, or made a short film, or something, to give them that bit of clout to beep an agent's radar. But once you do get representation, it's this guile and determination that will usually see you continuing to obtain work in some way or another while the agent will sort out the contract, and thus earn their 10%.

Your agent will work very hard for you and the remainder of their client list. They will tirelessly put your name forward for assignments or TV work and get your scripts onto the pile. They will do their best to arrange meetings with various producers/execs/commissioners. But none of this is a guarantee of work. You're making a mistake if you sit back waiting for your agent to phone or to organise meetings or to ask you to lunch. You've got to take on the same amount of promotion and marketing as your agent does.

Let's face it, they've got a lot of clients to punt and there's going to be that inevitable period of time when an agent has to wait for responses from the people they've sent your stuff to. While that happens, they can focus their attention on another client.

When you get an agent, don't expect too much. The excitement of getting an agent is great and the anticipation of professional work is stirring, but it may not happen right away. It takes time. It might feel like the next ice age is approaching by the time you get your first commission but at least you'll have hung in there, like a true pro, grafting and pitching and writing no matter what. The agent will continue to pitch you and your work, and you'll get meetings and be considered for various jobs; but after that, it's out of the agent's hands and you're left relying on lucky breaks, or someone taking a shine to your original voice or your unique brand of story material.

One thing's for sure, the amount of work, effort, determination, drive, sheer will and optimism that you have for yourself and your writing not only doubles but triples and quadruples as each  hurdle of rejection gets higher and higher. Having an agent as the positive coach on the side of the track urging you on is indispensable, but once you're in the race, it's all down to you and your personal resolve to be a success. Get ready to up your game to the next level, because the amount of effort you exert to succeed may seem like it's never enough.

Always be sniffing out opportunities, or making sure to introduce yourself to a producer/company who you want to meet or work with. This way, your relationship with your agent becomes a tag team of proactive endeavour.

You: "I've just set up a meeting with Lottie Amazement at Amazeballs, I sent her SuperSpec script and she really liked it."

Agent: "That's cool. I know Les Amazement at Amazeballs, I'll do a flag wave to make sure everyone knows you're coming in."

AGENTS

Some of the headlines from
this chapter

1 – Do you need one?

No. But they can help.

2 – Make a good approach

Any kind of hook is better than a blind
approach. Do some research first.

3 – Have a long-term strategy

Waiting for replies can take a while. So know
this will be a slow process.

4 – Continue reaching out

Carry on with your own proactive work in the
meantime – and even after you get an
agent.

TAKING CONTROL

What would Charlie Chaplin do?

Or rather, what would you say to Chaplin? You meet him at the pearly gates and he asks about what you did with the moving image in your time. "After all," he exclaims, "look at all the great technical advancements and opportunities that were available to you!"

* You had equipment at 1% of the price he did
* You had a way for your films to be seen by millions across the world without the need for expensive film prints
* You had sound, colour, editing
* Your film stock didn't catch fire
* You could do it anywhere in the world
* The edit suite fitted on a phone and you could edit on a train or even a plane

How many hundreds of films did you make? Maybe you (indeed, all of us) should feel the pressure of the great film pioneers so that we keep making stories.

Maybe we don't have a big budget. But we *can* make things, starting today. A script is just a stage in the making of a production – why not see that production through? That's what this chapter is about.

> 66
>
> *If you can't be expensive then be controversial.*
>
> 99
>
> **John Waters**
> Filmmaking legend

BEING A WRITER-HYPHEN

No one can be just a writer anymore!

We are often asked to give talks about the journey that some writers take – that of becoming a director. Here are our five tips.

* **1:** You already have a "director's vision". You have it as you write. Don't be scared of this term or think it means something special that's beyond your reach or talent level.

- **2**: Watch out for the "writer's disease", which is directing too closely to the script, pointing the camera at the dialogue all the time. Filming the speech isn't the best way. Hear the speech, see something else.

- **3**: Know the stages of production – now you have to see the film all the way through.

- **4**: Get ready for collaboration. You don't need to know everything technically, but you do need to know how to listen to people who know their stuff.

- **5**: Just do it. You can't learn this second hand. Like writing, you have to give it a go and take it from there.

> " *Before you direct you can be like: 'don't you dare touch my lovely words' – and then you get on set and it changes to 'these words are ruining my film'.* "
>
> **James Moran**

Becoming a writer-director is a common path, but one that's not suited to everyone. We feel there are two other equally good routes that writers could explore. One is becoming a producer, which gives you more power – you can fire the director! The second area is editing, as a lot of the skill set involved is similar to that of a writer.

REMEMBER
Don't wait to be invited

MAKE A SHORT

In this day and age, you need very little to make a short film. You can shoot and edit using your phone and computer. Or you can throw a bit of money at your production and borrow/hire a digital SLR camera, create homemade SFX, use your mates as actors, and bish bosh, you've got yourself a short. Or you can throw a decent amount of wedge into the film and try to make something that will stand out from the crowd, that will attract industry plaudits, and maybe even an award or two.

If you're thinking of making a short film, you might want to consider which of those three levels would suit you best.

Three levels of short film

No budget/Just for experience

This is the one where you'll shoot on anything. A camcorder, mobile phone, the video option on your digi-camera, or even using the built-in camera on your computer. Whatever. All you need to do is to write a script or a sketch that can accommodate a no-budget scenario, and away you go.

Some people like to skip this level. But we both recommend it. The reason is you don't know how to really edit a film until you shoot one. But until you've shot one, you can't edit it. Break the cycle by just knocking out a quickie!

A decent short

This is where you throw a bit more money in. Not much, but a little. It all depends on what you have available. It could be the cost of a night out, or a few hundred pounds (or is that the cost of a night out these days?). The point is to make something a bit more ambitious than the no-budget short. Something that's still fun and valuable but shows a bit more talent in front of and behind the camera. Something that might play at a smaller film festival, perhaps. Or do well online.

Professional short

An actual budget! Actors! Special effects! A crew of more than three people! Bingo, you're making a film! This is the one where you want to show people what you've got. You want to make a stylised, original short film that will wow the industry (winning short film festivals) and kick-start your career, or raise your profile at the very least.

Make the short that suits you best. But ensure it's a short that you want to make. There is no guarantee it will get into any festivals at all. But if you're proud of it, that helps in your promotion of the film over the long term.

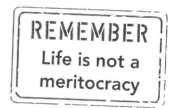

REMEMBER
Life is not a meritocracy

A lot of short films are shot on digital, at the weekend, with your mates, which is absolutely fine (see levels 1 and 2 above) but when Danny made his short, *Origin*, he was willing to throw a substantial amount of his own money (and raise some online, pre-Kickstarter) in order to have a budget that matched his ambition. As a result, the film screened in seven festivals – a decent run – and it won Best Horror at the London Independent Film Festival 2012.

See Danny's film *Origin*
http://www.originshortfilm.co.uk

OK, those are the key approaches. Now, the essential question: *How?*

Making a short film

Script

If you want to make a short film, you'll need a script. Good news is – you're a writer! Write one. Watch a lot of short films in the meantime. Get a feel for the stuff people are making: why it works, why it doesn't, why it won that film festival, etc. Shorts are hit and miss. A lot miss. You want to avoid that samey quality. Do something fun, original or distinctive, if at all possible. Pick a script that matches your budget level, too.

Budget

Decide how much you can spend, or how much you want to spend. Think about fundraising initiatives. A pub quiz. Ask all your friends/family for £20 each or whatever they can afford. Check out your local council for potential funds or investors. There are bits of money here, there and everywhere. It all adds up. But be realistic. How much would you give someone for their first or second short film? Not much. No complex scenes that you don't know how to pull off with what you have.

Cast and crew

Get help. But how do you get actors involved? What about crew? For actors, you approach their agents or get a casting director on board. Or get in touch with local drama and acting groups. For crew, you can trawl through Creative England's crew database (highly recommended), or get referrals/recommendations. Do a shout-out on Shooting People or the blogs or Twitter or on Facebook groups or whatever. People will generally respond to your passion and personality, as well as your script, and the cast and crew jigsaw will start to fall into place.

Just do it

If you think about it long enough, you'll convince yourself not to do it. Truth is, there's no excuse nowadays for *not* making a short film. Even if you're only vaguely interested, you could shoot a montage of stuff and play music over it, and you've got something to show your mates/family. It all depends on what you want to get out of it. There's no money to be made in short films. The audience barely exists. It's mainly for industry purposes, to showcase new talent. It's hard work. It's time-consuming. It's financially draining. But it's the best fun you can have with your clothes on (or y'know, off, if you're *that* kind of filmmaker). Whatever the case, get out there and make something.

Final note

Be sensible but challenging with your timescales. Getting the right cast and crew takes time. You can't organise a good short in a weekend. Likewise, setting a faraway deadline lacks urgency and means you put it off.

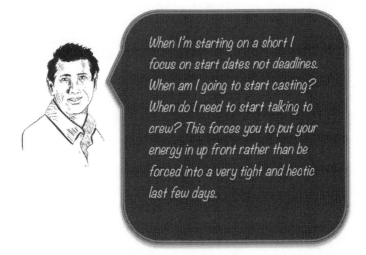

When I'm starting on a short I focus on start dates not deadlines. When am I going to start casting? When do I need to start talking to crew? This forces you to put your energy in up front rather than be forced into a very tight and hectic last few days.

" *Make sure your film feels inevitable. That it will be getting made and people need to join in right now or miss out.* "

Ted Hope
Producer
Adventureland, 21 Grams

LOW-BUDGET FEATURES

We shot our low-budget feature, *Who Killed Nelson Nutmeg?*, in the summer of 2014.

In many ways, low-budget features are the new shorts. A short film is highly unlikely to make money – or maybe these days it's actually impossible. But a low-budget feature can act as an industry calling card like a short does *and* may make some money back. And putting our producer's hat on for a moment, if our film makes a profit, it will definitely help to raise the budget for our next project.

The advice we gave for shorts works here, too – find cast and crew, and work to a sensible budget and timeframe – but there are a few things to add.

Schedule

Most successful low-budget features follow this pattern:

* script development = 6 months
* pre-production = 6 months (overlapping with script development)
* shoot = 1 month
* editing = 6 months
* sale of movie to biz = 6 months+

You can see it's quite a commitment of time. Hence a

few practice shorts are a good idea for your own sake! Even if you team up with more experienced people, your own learning is valuable, too.

Cameo name

It still helps to have a "name" in your cast. But it needs to be a suitable and on-topic name. For example, in *Who Killed Nelson Nutmeg?* (a kids' film) we had Bonnie Wright as our villain. She's best known as Ginny Weasley in the Harry Potter films. Our film's audience will be familiar with her, but we allowed her to play the bad "guy" for a change.

Script rewriting

Because we're writers we tend to overlook this element, rather ironically. We ask for help with crew, with acting, with editing, with every other element of the film. But because we know the craft of writing, we don't get help with the script. We should. Get some notes from a good script reader. It could be the best investment for your film. Fixing things when they're just words on a page is hundreds of times easier than fixing them on location or in the edit.

Our *Nelson Nutmeg* journey

In this book we can't cover the whole method of

shooting a low-budget feature. That would take an entire book in itself. In fact, there are many books already out there, including perhaps the most famous, *The Guerilla Filmmakers Handbook*.

But during the filmmaking process we had a few surprises and learnt some key lessons that don't seem to feature often in the various books we've seen.

Forget about the credit

Everyone wants to be the director, the big cheese, yes? But many years ago a very rich businessman gave us a tip. He said, "You can get whatever you want in life, so long as you don't want the credit." We think he's right. Our agreement was, let's co-write, co-direct, co-produce this to get it off the ground. Double our number of contacts, double the investment, share the work. Sometimes one of us does more than 50% of a certain job, and sometimes the other way around. We don't care. We are sharing the credit half-and-half and that's that. The bigger danger would be bickering about credits instead of doing good work. 50% of something awesome is better than 100% of something rubbish.

Don't focus on the script

You've got a good script, right? Or two? Or three? Great! But are they made? No. A good script isn't what's stopping you from making a feature right now. We realised this, and for the first three months of *Nelson Nutmeg* we had no script. That's right, we started casting, crewing and location hunting with no script at all, not even a rough draft. All we had was a treatment. Why did we do this? We knew we could write a decent script between us. That wasn't the main blocker. Having no money, no cast, no crew, no location – those were bigger blockers. First, we started work on removing those blockers. Do you still need a good script? Hell, yes. Do you have good scripts already in your archive? Maybe. Focus on the real reasons why you aren't shooting those scripts right now.

I've tried to get two really excellent features off the ground before. The scripts of both were pretty damn good, they did well in competitions and got good feedback. So clearly, the script wasn't what was stopping the films from happening. It was other reasons. So why repeat that mistake again?

Make lots of Kickstarter videos... *before* your Kickstarter campaign

No one knows about your film. They have never heard of it. They don't care. If you launch your crowdfunding campaign (like Kickstarter), you are using up your valuable 30 days trying to tell people about it. Instead of doing that, make lots of content first and spread the word. We had three months of Facebook and Twitter activity and also ten videos done *before* we launched.

More on Kickstarter and other crowdfunding later in this chapter.

Ignore successful films, but don't!

Most people's debut feature films are thrillers or horrors. Why? Because these genre films don't rely on big actors in order to be successful. But there are other genres that this idea also applies to. We chose a kids' film – with kids in the lead roles. Kind of like *The Goonies* or the Children's Film Foundation movies from the 60s and 70s. A film in this genre matched our profile and made sense. But it also meant we will only have to compete with about three other British films like this in the whole of the UK, in the whole of 2015.

Ignore successful films. But don't. The things you shouldn't ignore are the methods and techniques they used that made people want to see them and to recommend them to others. Sometimes we can be too smart for our own good and try to reinvent everything, instead of looking at a film that made a lot of money and that people liked and saying, well, let's do something like that.

Visit *Who Killed Nelson Nutmeg?* website
www.nelsonnutmeg.com
Twitter - @nelsonnutmeg

MAKE A DOCUMENTARY

Imagine going into a pitch meeting for your feature film

that focuses on an interesting group of characters who fought an exciting political campaign or cause. "Oh," says the commissioner, "that's an interesting story, I'd not heard of it and I'd like to know more." If you can, then pull out a 30-minute doc you've made on the subject – all the better.

With this approach, it's about creating a documentary in order to help move forward a fictional script that you have written and would like to see produced.

Some benefits of this approach:

▪ Bonus research: if you're doing primary research or interviews already, why not film them?

▪ Realistic practicalities: only a small crew needed. This way of working may suit the equipment and crew you have access to, more so than shooting an ambitious short film, for example.

▪ Passion and commitment: it shows potential funders and commissioners you have dedication to this story.

▪ Contacts and preparation: it demonstrates that you have access to key figures, locations or material.

▪ Immediate hook: it allows execs, funders and commissioners to easily understand your project better than a long, dry document could.

▪ Copyright to you: your self-made documentary acts as a copyrighted piece of work, staking your claim clearly with regards to a real-life event or story.

- Festival circuit: your documentary may be useful as a piece of work in its own right that you can enter into festivals, building the profile of both yourself and your drama script.
- Funding: you may be able to get some funding to expand or complete the documentary!
- Story and filmmaking: it forces you to think about the story approach on film as you edit the documentary.

66

Documentary should be closer to fiction and fiction should be closer to documentary. I make a documentary as part of my pre-production almost. By exploring the issues first hand and on film, I feel more confident to then move into a drama. Maybe we don't need to invent everything from nothing? For example, the first two people in Central Station are real people dictating real letters.

99

Walter Salles
Director

Being a factual piece, you may imagine there's nothing to bring from the storytelling craft to these projects. But there is. It's still a story, it's just a real story with real people. While you probably can't get involved in the finer points of dialogue, you can bring many elements of story structure into play.

A good documentary will probably answer these questions:

- Who are the heroes?
- What is their world?
- What adventure have they been called on?
- What barriers are getting in their way?
- Who is the villain? (The villain can be circumstance/external forces/internal emotions e.g. pride.)
- Will they overcome the barriers and defeat the villain?
- What in their personality helps them succeed? (Or is it by working together?)
- Will the world be changed after? For whom? For everyone?
- Can life go back to the old way? (Probably not, so what does the future look like?)

Not that squeezing all that in is easy, of course. But it acts as a guide when you get stuck.

STAGE A PLAY

Staging a play may cost about the same as making a short film. But it can be more effective in getting your story out into the world. We've already talked about writing for the theatre, but how about going further and actually producing a play?

Here are three benefits of putting on a play that you may not have considered:

* A play has similar constraints to a low-budget feature – minimal locations, 80 minutes long, small cast. A good play would usually be the equivalent of a good low-budget indie film.
* You can use it as a test reading of your film in many ways, finding out what works, what doesn't, what confuses people.
* People may review a play. Hardly anyone reviews short films. A review quote from *Time Out* will be pretty handy in your feature film pitch.

One word of caution: if you're thinking of this as a way to work on a feature film or TV drama idea, then make sure the audience can't see that ambition. This needs to work 100% as a play in its own right. You're adapting it to a different medium. Characters may go, scenes may be revised accordingly – be bold.

Hire a venue (a room above a pub, that kind of thing), get some actors, invite your friends and you have your first staged production.

If you want to do it for experience rather than to progress an existing idea, then putting a modern or comedic spin on a familiar idea/story (that isn't copyright) is a good way to get the punters in. Even better, write to the original author and get their permission to adapt their script/book/film into your play. They'll probably say no but they might say yes. When Danny was a researcher in TV, his golden rule was always ask, otherwise you'll never know ("actually, even now as a jobbing writer, that's what I always do!").

GETTING FUNDING

Official sources of funding change all the time. It would be crazy to put them in a book. But we're crazy. Here's the state of play as of going to press. Assume two facts:

One: That all this info is out of date and you must do your own research.

Two: That you won't get any funding ever. See it as a bonus, rather than at the core of your production strategy.

BFI

The BFI hands out the largest amount to filmmakers, from short films, to feature development, production, post-production and distribution.

The BFI's funding page
http://www.bfi.org.uk/supporting-uk-film/funding-filmmakers

Regions

Wales, Northern Ireland, Scotland and England all have their own funding bodies, too. Creative England is perhaps the most well known as they fund iFeatures which develops and funds films for around £350k. Most of the regions fund short films and docs, too.

Creative England
http://www.creativeengland.co.uk/film

Creative Scotland
http://www.creativescotland.com/funding

Ffilm – Wales
http://www.ffilmcymruwales.com

Northern Ireland Screen
http://www.northernirelandscreen.co.uk/

Other funders

MEDIA Desk funding

The MEDIA Programme offers many different funding schemes, each targeting different areas of the audiovisual sector.

Visit the MEDIA funding page
http://www.mediadeskuk.eu/funding/

Creative Skillset

Creative Skillset (used to be known simply as Skillset) manages a range of training funds.

Find funding for better training
http://creativeskillset.org/who_we_help/creative_profession

British Council Shorts Support Scheme

For financial and promotional assistance in submitting short films to key film festivals around the world.

See how the British Council could help you
http://film.britishcouncil.org/our-projects/on-going-projects/shorts-support-scheme

CROWDFUNDING

Free money! But why would anyone give you money?

This section is about crowdsourcing or crowdfunding. The popular sites for this are Kickstarter and Indiegogo. But there are others.

In the past, we would have a whip-round. Now we crowdfund. There are a lot of producers trying to raise money in this way for their films, but we see three trends that are working above all others.

With each example we have tried to outline what the investor gets back – **at an emotional level**. All films offer things such as *"a signed copy if you invest $50"*. But the real, emotional reason to invest is often different.

Type 1 – Super gloss for nerds

These films tend to be about the showmanship of cinema, they give you a chance to fund a spectacle. This taps into two emotions. The first is the "being part of something bigger" feeling. This is the same emotional need that made rich patrons invest in large gladiator fights in Rome. You want to be part of something you could never do yourself.

The second feeling is harder to define. We can only call

it "a boasting of knowledge". This is because you can follow the development of the film. Show it to people. And then tell them lots of details about it only you know. It's like the ultimate collector's edition, and a chance for you to show off!

Type 2 – A cause

These films are more about the cause that the film represents: an issue, a philosophy or an approach to life.

Georgia van Cuylenburg made a film about alopecia, and attracted interest from people who were involved with the condition, rather than solely having an interest in documentary films in general.

Here the emotional reason for investing is clear – it's about doing something. It's about getting a film out there on an issue, when perhaps there seems little else proactive that can be done.

Type 3 – A link to a bigger audience

Can your film link to something wider? A genre maybe. Or fans of a band whose music is featured. Anything that can broaden your appeal beyond the people you know.

Our own Kickstarter

We managed a successful Kickstarter campaign for *Who Killed Nelson Nutmeg?*

Here's what we did (a very simple method):

- Emailed everyone we knew personally.
- Wrote daily/frequent updates on Facebook, Twitter, Facebook groups, LinkedIn groups and sometimes Reddit.
- Uploaded video updates every few days.
- Approached magazines and blogs to interview us, or publish guest articles.
- Asked for as little as £1 from people. Having many contributors giving a little each is better than a few giving larger amounts – the algorithms on Kickstarter push it up the charts quicker. People feel better about chipping in if it's like this. Asking for a single quid is easy too, if you're shy of asking for money. Most people will give more anyway once they check out your rewards.
- Built a lot of the campaign around the genre of children's film.
- Focused on our aim to make a kids' film with kids in it – a kind of cause for people to get behind.

Using online methods to spread the word and gain attention for your film is great. But don't forget the old "real world" methods, too. Only a few years ago you would see people in Cannes dressing up, making up gimmicks, handing out flyers – anything to draw people in. The last time Tim went to Cannes, he didn't see anyone do this. The time is ripe to bring this kind of showmanship back. After all, it will be easy to stand out if there's no competition.

Seedrs

Seedrs enables you to attract investment in rather than donations to your project. People are getting a share in your production. The benefit to this is that you can raise much larger amounts; in fact it has to if it's to pay for itself as a method. This approach would normally be for people on their second or third feature, or with a proven track record. One to bookmark for later perhaps, rather than pursue as your first crowdfunding project.

Seedrs
https://www.seedrs.com

BEWARE THE DOPPLER EFFECT

Two warnings about all these ideas…

Let things sit

A sound wave "sounds" different depending on if it's travelling towards you or away from you. The most commonly used example of this phenomenon is an ambulance siren, which will change pitch as it flies past you. This is called the Doppler Effect and, simply put, is an explanation of how wavelengths change if relative speed changes.

What's this got to do with filmmaking? Replace "siren" with "idea".

A new idea can be distorted if it comes at you quickly. The speed of its approach to your mind distorts it and makes it sound better (or worse) than it might actually be. Let it sit for a while first. Only an idea that has been processed for a while can be judged as being pitch-perfect or not.

Next time you get that flash of inspiration, enjoy it – then remember the Doppler Effect. This is true for script ideas *and* fundraising ideas.

Don't let talking replace doing

Talking about a project too much can actually take

away your desire to do it! The excitement that you should get once you've completed the project comes early. Talking about it is as exciting as doing it.

People often write scripts or make films because they want to say something and share their love of an idea. Sharing that with too many people before completion may mean they feel it's mission accomplished and they take their foot off the pedal.

The same applies to crowdfunding. The energy that goes into getting the funding and the excitement of reaching the target can in fact steal some of the dedication needed to produce the actual film.

TAKING CONTROL

Have a go at creating...

1 – A short film

At the right level of complexity to suit you.

2 – A low-budget feature

More work than a short, but more profitable.

3 – A documentary

Prove the theme of your film is interesting.

4 – A play

Get live audience feedback on your stories.

BONUS TIP

Don't forget we've already said that you could write and produce your own comic book or web series.

THE LONG HAUL

This final chapter is about keeping going. Most people don't have a break-out success. Or a break-*in* success. How do you keep going in a sure and steady manner? And what changes await you as you progress and get better?

REMEMBER
There is
no 'inside'

" *Why do we do all this? Why tell stories? Cinema and storytelling is there to smash the jail that we've put ourselves in.* "

Anthony Minghella
Writer and Director
Cold Mountain, The English Patient

DEALING WITH REJECTION

There's no denying that rejection sucks, and it hurts, and it's very personal (to us; it's never a personal decision from the person rejecting you), but it's how you dust yourself off and keep writing that will determine whether you can cut it in the biz. You'll need a steely resolve, a desire to improve, the belief that you can make it, that you really do have talent, and the humility to accept that you might not succeed, despite having all the necessary qualities to do so.

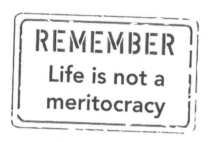

REMEMBER
Life is not a
meritocracy

There's a fine line between determination and delusion, unfortunately. You can tell yourself, "I'm gonna make it, no matter what", and have all the will in the world, and perhaps even some talent, but the chips may not fall your way and the effects can be damaging.

'Successful writers have one thing in common, they didn't give up'. It's a popular motivational quote, but it wasn't *just* their desire to succeed that got them where they are today. They knew that they had what it takes, and nobody was going to stop them from writing. For most writers, talent and determination will get them so far, but it's Lady Luck who will have a strong say on which side of the fence they fall.

It's a point worth reiterating that making a living as a screenwriter is going to take time. It's not going to happen overnight, or within a few months. You'll be extremely lucky if it happens within a few years.

If you're in it for the money, forget it, it's not going to happen. There is good money to be made but it's not just handed out willy-nilly. You have to earn your place in the system, and work hard for your reward. In the early days of your career, if you're lucky enough to get a few breaks, the money won't be regular, and it will be a struggle to survive. That's when you realise that even when you're "making it", it's still just as hard as before, if not harder, as you have to maintain momentum, create more stories and find more work.

There is one positive about rejection. It means you're doing the right activity. You're writing, and sending your scripts out into the world. Rejection is the norm, but some knock-backs are more crushing than others. They will make you question whether you want to continue, and poke you with nagging doubts about your talent. It takes a brave person to know when they've been beaten, and to hang up their spurs. It takes a braver one to continue, knowing that they're going to make it. Some day.

REMEMBER
Be in it for
the long term

> *When you've got your head down in a draft, got a really tight deadline, you've got to remind yourself that a week ago, this was all you ever wanted to do.*

Sophie Petzal
Writer
Wolfblood, Danger Mouse, Jekyll & Hyde

DEVELOPING YOURSELF

Have you seen the episode of *The Simpsons* where Homer gets his arm stuck in a drinks vending machine? Eventually the fire department arrives. For them, there is no choice – they have to cut off his arm. But at the last minute a fireman looks through a small crack in the front of the machine.

> FIREMAN
> Homer, are you just holding onto the can?

> HOMER
> Your point being?

Are you holding onto a can because you want to? Even though you know they will cut your arm off? Are you still holding onto a can that says "an agent will get me work" or "film is better than TV"? Let go of the can!

Ongoing development can sometimes be about what to *stop* doing, as much as learning new things to *start* doing.

WHAT IS YOUR NEW HOBBY?

Your writing probably started out more as a hobby. You made films for fun maybe, with your mates, for a laff!

Now it's become more like work. You want to do it "properly" and "make a go of it". It isn't your hobby anymore. Except it is. Because you love doing it – you do it as work *and* as a hobby.

BUT – when do you switch off? When do you do something else? What is it?

Not tackling this question is something we have seen too often before from too many people (including ourselves!). An obsessive drive about writing creates tiredness at best, burnout at worst.

The most successful people, people doing the most interesting work, have a kind of magic ingredient. Yes, they're good at writing (or directing, or whatever their profession is) and they also have a good life, or lived an interesting one, and draw inspiration from that.

But then there is their hobby (or hobbies!). This is what makes them different. It makes them more than "just another writer". Their pastimes give them the ability to switch off and have fun – clear the mind! – but they also provide ongoing perspective and insight about their work. It might sound a bit corny but it's true.

We're actually telling you not to write every now and then: get a hobby!

KEEP FEEDING YOUR MIND

Sometimes we need to get our heads out of our own industry. If we don't, then we may be on the path to postmodernism gone mad, and regurgitating old ideas.

It's important to step outside of our narrow artistic view, think about the wider world and see what's going on in other art forms. And by art forms we mean cartoons, comics, novels, games – whatever you like.

Look around. See how others are pushing back the boundaries and then compare this activity to your own work. Integrate it. Use it. Be inspired by it.

CIRCLE OF COLLEAGUES

Over time you should develop a strong circle of colleagues and peers – business friends, if you like to think of them in that way (or "frolleagues" as Danny calls them).

This is not only for moral support or to share advice and contacts, but also to share raw ideas and early drafts. Ordinarily, you wouldn't want to share those with other people in the business. But if you have a core group of fellow writers who understand the writing process and can also offer a creative solution to whatever problem you're experiencing, you'll find yourself spending less time going down dead ends.

This circle of colleagues could be local to you, but

could also be virtual – or a mix of both.

> **❝**
>
> *There are more web links than there are neural connections in your brain. So share your ideas and put them out there.*
>
> *The moment of genius in your mind is when you join up two seemingly unconnected thoughts suddenly in a new way.*
>
> *But what if you have half the idea in your brain and the other half is in someone else's? Well, that's why I invented the web.* **❞**

Tim Berners-Lee
Inventor of the World Wide Web

A MENTOR

A mentor is an industry figure who can guide you through some tricky situations or new career experiences. There are some formal mentoring schemes run by the various funding bodies which can pair you up with seasoned pros. But there's nothing to stop you reaching out to people yourself. In fact, it's often better. The formal schemes usually have a set timetable (for example, meeting once a month for six months) but that schedule may not suit your project. If you arrange your own mentor, the process can be more about what works for you both.

You can also think about a project-specific mentor. We asked Nigel Cole, director of *Calendar Girls* and *Made In Dagenham*, to be our mentor for *Who Killed Nelson Nutmeg?* Although we had both directed in the past, this was our first feature and it was terrific to have Nigel to offer advice – and all because Danny reached out to him on Twitter!

TIME MANAGEMENT

The good news about time is that no one has an advantage over you. The Coen Brothers don't have more time than you. William Goldman doesn't. Chaplin didn't. As struggling writers, we can at least take a quantum of solace from that. How do we get the most out of our time?

Most time management models are written by companies looking to squeeze more effort out of workers for the same money. What should you do to manage time yourself – and keep a good balance?

And before we get too deep into time management,

consider how much of a fib it is as a title. You can't manage time. It happens at the same speed whatever you do (General Relativity aside).

Here are three very simple tips for completing the marathon of writing and filmmaking:

1 – Bitesize it

Like the old adage, how do you eat an elephant? One bite at a time. Just break it down into tasks. To do x pages, or whatever suits you. Then do it.

2 – Block out time in healthy chunks

We find some people spend more time switching between tasks than actually doing them. Time studies have shown that it's better to do one job thoroughly than chop and change about. Finding the block of time that works for you is key. For us, this is two hours.

Small addition to this: some people never start anything because they want a full day in order to really get into it. And that full day never arrives. In fact, you can do a lot in 30 minutes.

3 – Make it tasty

Have something to aim for as a motivator. Whatever turns you on, baby. Have something to look forward to, as a reward for finishing.

Longer term

How do you keep a balance long term? Remember the Scriptwriter's Life diagram? Using that as a guide, you could set yourself three goals each day – do some work, find some work, feed your brain.

LASER BEAM IT!

Danny once had a meeting with his agent, a general catch-up of what was happening, and what writing plans were ahead. The agent said something offhand, almost as a bad joke, but it stuck with Danny as a great piece of advice: "Laser beam it!"

What she meant was, focus on *one area/genre that you're particularly good at*, and put all your effort into that (especially if it's providing income).

If you're great at writing supernatural thrillers, be *the* supernatural thriller guy/gal. Establish yourself in that genre, don't do anything else, become the expert.

If you're really into writing romcoms but find you have a flair for writing for kids' TV, then focus on writing for kids' TV. You'll earn money and build a decent profile, then you can stretch out and write your romcoms.

Essentially, "laser beam it" means that sometimes what we want to do is not necessarily the best path to pursue. This doesn't mean that we should completely ignore our creative passions and instincts; it just means that if you find yourself getting work in one particular area, and are good at it, then reap as much as you can.

Bottom line: write whatever you want, but when it comes to commissions and earning money, write what the industry thinks you're best at writing. Find your particular talent and genre, then *laser beam it!*

THE LONG HAUL

Stick at it by...

1 – Coping with rejection
It isn't personal.

2 – Developing yourself
Focus on your emotional well-being. What is your new hobby?

3 – Mastering time management
Time slips away easily. Put together a system that works for you.

4 – Getting support
Find an industry mentor you can turn to for difficult questions. They will have made the mistakes already! Or use a range of peers.

5 – Laser beam it!
Focus on what you're good at.

FADE OUT

REMEMBER...

1 – Be in it for the long term

Everything takes time in the writing world because of the complexity and size of the projects. Plan for that.

2 – It's a small industry

Word gets around if you are a pain to work with. Get to know people and like them for who they are, not what they can do for you.

3 – There is no "inside"

An industry is just the people who work within it. Focus on seeing the talented colleagues around you, not a monolith of "the business".

4 – Do it your way, today

Our way won't be your way. Think about what you can do with your own unique situation.

5 – Don't wait to be invited

People like to work with "doers", so get proactive and start making things happen.

6 – Life is not a meritocracy

Many circumstances steer a career. Don't take setbacks personally.

7 – Think about the other side

How would you like to be treated? Do that.

BE...

- Practical.
- Proactive.
- Professional.

And don't forget to have patience!

OUR FINAL MESSAGE

In *The Big Bang Theory*, Leonard's mom comes to visit and states, "I've been responsible for my own orgasms since 1982." Good for her. Of course she didn't say it, the writers did! In this case some combination of Chuck

Lorre, Bill Prady, David Goetsch, Lee Aronsohn, Steven Molaro, Richard Rosenstock and Maria Ferrari.

The point here is, we are responsible for our own careers – and for surviving them!

If it all feels crap, sort it out. It's your fault it's crap and it's your responsibility to fix it. You're the writer. This is your life. You've chosen it.

We know the hero's journey so well that we believe it must be true, that we will conquer adversity and win the day. But we can't all be the central role, can we? Do the best you can in your own unique situation.

Other people, normal people, can moan about their office, about their work, about how their career wasn't what they wanted.

Don't be like that. **Don't just survive – thrive!**

ACKNOWLEDGEMENTS

This book is an effort to collate all our experience over the years into a practical handbook. First, a big thank you to the readers of our blogs and the listeners of the UK Scriptwriters podcast. We think it's important to share information, and without your feedback and support we wouldn't have done this book. Indeed, if there's something that's not covered or if you have a specific question, then feel free to get in touch: ukscriptwriters@hotmail.com

Special thanks to Emily Gilbert for her lovely illustrations, and our copy-editor Jo-Ann Challis, who helped us find a common voice for the book.

Thanks, too, to all the writers whose wit and wisdom has featured in the book. Some of them we know, some of them we've met, some of them we'd love to meet and thank personally:

* Tim Berners-Lee
* Doug Chamberlin
* Richard Dinnick
* Andrew Ellard
* Phil Ford
* Mike Garley
* Yvonne Grace
* Tom Green
* James Henry
* Chris Hill

- Ted Hope
- Mark Huckerby
- Tony Jordan
- Michelle Lipton
- Barbara Machin
- Guy Maddin
- Anthony Minghella
- Debbie Moon
- James Moran
- Chris Musselwhite
- Nick Ostler
- Steve Pemberton
- Sophie Petzal
- Rob Pratten
- Lord David Puttnam
- Walter Salles
- Reece Shearsmith
- Suki Singh
- Iain Softley
- Georgia van Cuylenburg
- John Waters

Printed in Great Britain
by Amazon